THE
COMMUNICATION
STRATEGY
HANDBOOK

This book is part of the Peter Lang Media and Communication list.
Every volume is peer reviewed and meets
the highest quality standards for content and production.

PETER LANG
New York • Bern • Berlin
Brussels • Vienna • Oxford • Warsaw

BETTEKE VAN RULER
FRANK KÖRVER

THE COMMUNICATION STRATEGY HANDBOOK

Toolkit for
Creating a Winning Strategy

PETER LANG
New York • Bern • Berlin
Brussels • Vienna • Oxford • Warsaw

Library of Congress Cataloging-in-Publication Data

Names: Ruler, Betteke van, author. | Körver, Frank, author.
Title: The communication strategy handbook: toolkit for creating a winning
strategy / Betteke van Ruler and Frank Körver.
Other titles: Strategisch communicatie frame. English
Description: New York: Peter Lang, 2019.
Includes bibliographical references.
Identifiers: LCCN 201804467 | ISBN 978-1-4331-5483-6 (hardback: alk. paper)
ISBN 978-1-4331-5657-1 (paperback: alk. paper) | ISBN 978-1-4331-5658-8 (ebook pdf)
ISBN 978-1-4331-5659-5 (epub) | ISBN 978-1-4331-5660-1 (mobi)
Subjects: LCSH: Communication in management. | Communication in organizations.
Classification: LCC HD30.3 .R8513 2019 | DDC 658.4/5—dc23
LC record available at https://lccn.loc.gov/2018044677
DOI 10.3726/b13518

Bibliographic information published by **Die Deutsche Nationalbibliothek.**
Die Deutsche Nationalbibliothek lists this publication in the "Deutsche
Nationalbibliografie"; detailed bibliographic data are available
on the Internet at http://dnb.d-nb.de/.

Concept and text
Betteke van Ruler
Frank Körver

Design and artwork
Bianca Spierenburg, studiopolkadot.nl

Project management
Frank Jansen, DtC | Desire to Communicate

Editing
Peter Lang Publishing, Inc.

Translation
Elizabeth Manton
Taalcentrum-VU

Photography
Phil Nijhuis
Sjaak Ramakers

Originally published in Dutch: *Het strategisch communicatie frame:*
Praktische methode voor strategie-ontwikkeling © 2014 Betteke van Ruler and Frank Körver

CONTENTS

CONTENTS

CONTENTS

CONTENTS

ACKNOWLEDGEMENTS

Writing this book on communication strategy is an effort of many people over many years.

For their support we want to express our sincere thanks to the corporate communication professionals who inspired us to further develop our ideas on communication strategy development and write this book.

We also wish to pay tribute to all Dutch communication professionals who have extensively experimented with the preliminary versions of the Communication Strategy Framework method. Without their enthusiasm, support, and valuable feedback the method could not have matured into the highly practical tool as it did.

This book is enriched with exciting thoughts on strategy development. For their special statements on this subject we want to express our gratitude to professor **Paul A. Argenti** (USA), professor **Xianhong Chen** (China), professor **Maria Aparecida Ferrari** (Brazil), professor **Larissa Grunig** (USA), professor **Robert Heath** (USA), professor **Jim Macnamara** (Australia), professor **Ángeles Moreno** (Spain), professor **Ronél Rensburg** (South Africa), professor **Dejan Verčič** (Slovenia), **Stephen Waddington** (UK), **Inge Wallage** (The Netherlands), and professor **Ansgar Zerfass** (Germany). We feel privileged for having been able to add their personal contributions to this book. They teach us so much about communication strategy development.

Finally, the authors want to thank Peter Lang, New York, for the publication of the book, and particularly Production Manager Jackie Pavlovic for guiding us through the process from manuscript to the book you hold.

THE ESSENCE OF STRATEGY IS CHOOSING WHAT NOT TO DO

- Michael Porter, 2011, p. 20

WHY
A COMMUNICATION
STRATEGY
FRAMEWORK?

THE COMMUNICATION STRATEGY FRAMEWORK HAS BEEN DESIGNED TO HELP PROFESSIONALS MAKE TARGETED CHOICES. HOWEVER, RATHER THAN PRE-SCRIBE A SPECIFIC COURSE OF ACTION OR THE BEST STRATEGY, WHICH IS ALWAYS CONTEXT-DEPENDENT, THE FRAMEWORK GUIDES YOU TO ASK THE RIGHT QUESTIONS AND TO EVALUATE WHAT YOUR ORGANIZATION, CLIENT, OR PROJECT REALLY NEEDS. IT COMPELS YOU TO THINK ABOUT HOW COMMUNICATION CAN CONTRIBUTE TO ACHIEVING YOUR ORGANIZATION'S OR CLIENT'S PRIORITIES OR YOUR PROJECT GOALS.

The Communication Strategy Framework is a planning method wholly different to the classic step-by-step plan still common in the worlds of public relations and corporate communication, of which John Marston's widely used RACE model is one example.

We don't really believe in plans of that type. Rather than showing which choices you have made and why you made them, their main function is to outline intended actions and what those actions will accomplish, and are strongly focused on control. The Communication Strategy Framework, by contrast, is an agile method that enables you to continually adapt to changing circumstances while staying in command. By now we both have quite a bit of experience in working with the Communication Strategy Framework, and we feel it to be a very rewarding method——as, do many other professionals!

This book was first published in the Netherlands, in Dutch, in 2014. Although we knew our method fulfilled a need, the wide enthusiasm with which it was embraced not only by public relations and corporate communication professionals but also, thanks to its broad applicability, in other fields such as human relations, marketing, and general management, was beyond what we could have dreamed. Indeed, as of 2018, the Communication Strategy Framework is used by virtually all communication professionals in the Netherlands, and the model is also taught at many universities. Therefore, we deemed the time was ripe for an English translation.

Innovation is not only about creating things that are new, but also about exploring new ways of doing things. Our Communication Strategy Framework invites you, the reader, to explore an alternative method of strategy development:

> IF YOU CANNOT DESCRIBE YOUR STRATEGY IN ONE MINUTE, IT'S NOT A SOLID STRATEGY

- by explicitly considering external alongside internal contexts based on your specific communication vision and gauging their relative importance
- by intensifying your collaboration with key players, both internal and external
- by making choices that may be more drastic than usual, aided by the incisive questions this book forces you to ask—and answer
- by taking your organization's objectives as your starting point, though without letting them define you
- by taking an iterative approach and continually reflecting on whether your choices remain congruent.

And all the while asking a fundamental question: How can communication genuinely make the difference?

Strategy development is one of the most daunting challenges facing any professional, no matter the field. After all, the stakes are high. Developing effective strategies can put you on the path to becoming a trusted advisor and a valued member of the organization, but the process itself is complex and labor-intensive. However, this does not excuse anyone who has mapped out a strategy from the obligation to be able to explain it clearly. If you cannot describe in five minutes what you want to do, why you want to do it, how you will do it, and who and what you need to get it done, then it's not a solid strategy. Articulating these aspects clearly is in itself a big challenge. The Framework can help you do it.

Where classic communication plans can extend to dozens if not hundreds of pages, our preferred method of strategy development employs sticky notes and a big sheet of paper tacked on the wall. Using this approach, the Communication Strategy Framework instantly shows you whether your choices line up and whether the choices you have made in the Framework's various building blocks are actually congruent with each other.

Once you know how the Communication Strategy Framework works and have learned to use it, you will be rewarded with visible results. You'll be able to make clear to anyone which choices you have made and which actions you plan to take, and therefore to get vital input. You will be able to align your choices with priorities elsewhere in the organization, and also to claim your role within it.

This book was developed and written by Betteke van Ruler, with the exception of the chapters "High Requirements, Rising Expectations" and "Business Focused Communication," which were written by Frank Körver. Frank additionally contributed a wealth of practical insights to Betteke's sections and supplied the kickstarters, do's and don'ts, and the case example. This blend of theory and practice has resulted in a book packed with valuable and useful information.

In setting out this method, this book invites you to take a new approach to strategy development and to present the results of that development process in a more effective way. We encourage you to experiment with the model, apply it, and to share your experiences with others. We hope you will find it as rewarding as we do!

For the sake of simplicity and readability, this book mainly uses the terms "communication professional" and "communication department." These should be understood to refer equally to communication, public relations, and public affairs teams and agencies, corporate communication and agile teams and tribes, or whatever analogous term fits your context.

Betteke van Ruler and **Frank Körver**

April 2019

P.S. We would love to hear what you think of the Communication Strategy Framework. Please do write to let us know!
Betteke van Ruler: *ruler@telfort.nl*; Frank Körver: *frank.korver@wepublic.nl*

THE COMMUNICATION STRATEGY FRAMEWORK: A PRACTICAL METHOD

WHY A GOOD COMMUNICATION STRATEGY IS VITAL

- Planning is always essential. But nowadays planning is not simply about deter-mining a sequence of steps. More and more, planning requires intelligent prag-matism and flexibility. Only then can you add real value. A good strategy creates scope for pragmatism and agility.

- We live in a fast-paced world. We want to take enough time for things that are important, but often that is a luxury we just don't have. Strategic choices there-fore have to be crystal clear. A good strategy cuts to the core and can be ex-plained in a page or less. If it cannot, you have not been critical enough. Strategy is about making choices, and excelling is about making choices that make a dif-ference.

- Communication can put your organization on the road to success, but only if you are doing the right things the right way—and showing it. Accountability is key: a good communication strategy enlarges your accountability.

- A communication strategy with no support beyond the communication depart-ment is doomed to fail. How you make strategic choices can be just as important as the strategic choices themselves. A good communication strategy, based on logical choices, generates support and enthusiasm among internal and external stakeholders.

- Senior management are not the only ones to set a high bar for communicati-on. Most communication professionals are ambitious too. These days, nobody wants another "armchair expert." The stakes are too high. A good communica-tion strategy is an essential proof of your ability to deliver.

The Communication Strategy Framework offers a practical method for creating effective strategies. Our method enables you to plan an approach, set priorities, and make the right choices. That, in a nutshell, is the Strategic Communication Framework. It does not prescribe a course of action or tell you which strategy is best; rather, it helps you to ask the right questions and to evaluate what your organization, client, or project really needs, and forces you think about where communication serves a real purpose. It helps you to make choices about who and what are needed to achieve your ambitions. And, last but not least, it brings you another step closer to being accountable and claiming your role in the organization.

RETHINK YOUR APPROACH

The Communication Strategy Framework is a planning method that is wholly different to the classic step-by-step plan. Where the old approach is static and focused on control, the Communication Strategy Framework offers you a new way to think about strategy development by:

- explicitly considering the internal and external contexts based on your communication vision and gauging their relative importance
- intensifying your collaboration with key players
- making choices that may be more drastic than usual—and critically re-evaluating those choices periodically
- taking your organization's objectives as the starting point
- taking an iterative approach.

All the while asking this fundamental question: How can communication make the difference?

STRATEGY DEVELOPMENT AS A CONTINUOUS PROCESS

A strategic approach is expressed in the actions you take day to day. Are those actions relevant? But what is relevant? The answer may be less obvious than it seems. Relevance is not determined by the latest craze or personal preferences. Those are not relevant. The Communication Strategy Framework helps you to reflect on what you want to do and to ask the right questions in order to then make the most effective choices. Beyond that, it helps you to visualize your goal on a day-to-day basis and to evaluate whether you are still focused on the right things. What it also shows is that strategy is never set in stone. If it turns out that a choice you made is no longer relevant, this will almost certainly impact your other choices, too. Strategy development is a continuous process.

AGILITY VERSUS LINEARITY

HOW TO MAKE CHANGE A ROUTINE PART

Martin Reeves and Mike Deimler (2011) stress that we live in an era of risk and instability. Uncertainty poses a tremendous challenge for strategy making. We agree with them that traditional methods of strategy development are over. Traditional approaches to strategy development assume a stable and predictable world, and our world is everything but stable and predictable, they claim. Organizations need to move quicker and smarter. In order to adapt to a continuously changing environment, they will have to change their way of thinking. And they need to adopt a new way of working as well.

PWC (2012) as well as many other consultancy firms favor the so-called agile organization. The agile organization strives to make change a routine part of organizational life to reduce or eliminate the organizational trauma that paralyzes many businesses attempting to adapt to new markets and environments. Because change is perpetual, they claim, the agile enterprise is able to nimbly adjust to and take advantage of emerging opportunities. Agile stands for flexible, smart, fast, and result-oriented. The hallmark for agile is learning; agile organizations are learning organizations, as Belinda Waldock states in *Being Agile in Business* (2015). One simple tool you definitely need for agile working is sticky notes. By their nature they are flexible and easy to use; groups of notes can easily be reviewed by the group, and they can help you to work together and start the discussion on choices to be made. A more important aspect of agile is active listening. To the co-creators of your strategy, to your clients and managers, and to all the people you have to listen to in order to develop an effective strategy. The Communication Strategy Framework can help you to work in an agile way.

ALL TOO LINEAR

In the various editions of his well-known book *Strategic Planning for Public Relations*, Ronald D. Smith suggests that the planning process in public relations consists of four phases, with all together nine steps. The first phase is analysis of the situation, the organization, and the publics. The second is to draw up a strategic plan, which means establishing goals and objectives, formulating action and response strategies, and developing the message strategy. The third phase is tactics, which means first selecting communication tactics, and then implementing the strategic plan. The fourth phase is evaluation of the plan. This method is also known as RACE: Research, Action plan, Communications, Evaluation.

In this kind of traditional communication planning you determine beforehand what results you want to achieve and what actions you must perform to arrive there. You set your targets and tactics all in advance. When conditions change along the way, or when the effects of your actions prove to be different to what you expected, you are forced to admit that your goals were not realistic, that you aimed for the wrong target, and/or that you did not choose the right strategy, the right actions, or the right message. In short, that it was a waste of money and time.

That is why we must change our method of strategy-building in public relations and corporate communication and make it more agile, oriented toward choices instead of actions.

AGILE PRACTITIONERS
The Communication Strategy Framework is all about reflecting and adjusting. An agile method demands agile professionals. Although not called agile, the idea of re- flecting and adjusting as the best way to act is far from new.

REFLECTIVE ACTION MODEL
In 1946 Kurt Lewin published a fre- quently cited article in which he argued that real professionals conti- nuously reflect on their actions. He was referring to professionals wor- king with minorities, but this applies equally to other professionals. The core idea is that every action must lead to observation of the reaction and to reflection on it, thus benefi- ting the planning for the following ac- tion. This is equivalent to the idea of testing and refinement in agility. You might be familiar with the PDCA mo- del of W. Edwards Deming. That, too, is based on the action research model of Kurt Lewin.

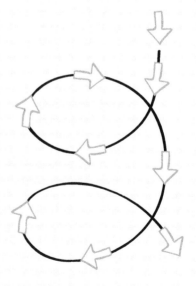

Figure 1. Lewin's Reflective Action Model

THE COMMUNICATION STRATEGY FRAMEWORK

Strategy is all about making choices

STRATEGY

STRATEGY IS ABOUT MAKING CHOICES

'THE BIG LIE OF STRATEGIC PLANNING'

"All executives know that strategy is important. But almost all also find it scary, because it forces them to confront a future they can only guess at. Worse, actually choosing a strategy entails making decisions that explicitly cut off possibilities and options. An executive may well fear that getting those decisions wrong will wreck his or her career.

The natural reaction is to make the challenge less daunting by turning it into a problem that can be solved with tried and tested tools. That nearly always means spending weeks or even months preparing a comprehensive plan for how the company will invest in existing and new assets and capabilities in order to achieve a target—an increased share of the market, say, or a share in some new one. The plan is typically supported with detailed spreadsheets that project costs and revenue quite far into the future. By the end of the process, everyone feels a lot less scared.

This is a truly terrible way to make strategy. It may be an excellent way to cope with fear of the unknown, but fear and discomfort are an essential part of strategy-making. In fact, if you are entirely comfortable with your strategy, there's a strong chance it is not very good. (...) You need to be uncomfortable and apprehensive: True strategy is about placing bets and making hard choices. The objective is not to eliminate risk but to increase the odds of success."

From:
Roger L. Martin, 2014, p. 78

EVERY ORGANIZATION, EVERY DEPARTMENT, EVERY TEAM, AND EVERY PROJECT NEEDS A STRATEGY TO ACHIEVE IMPACT. WITHOUT STRATEGY, YOU RUN THE RISK BEING RULED BY FADS OR GOING FROM TASK TO TASK WITHOUT MAKING A REAL DIFFERENCE.

DOING THE RIGHT THING

Something we see quite a lot is CEOs who are eager to make their corporate communication "more strategic" and communication directors who push their teams to "think more strategically." Usually, their motivation is to get the communication department to contribute more to organizational targets, but at minimal cost.

There is nothing wrong with this. However, zooming in on strategy often causes people to lose sight of the business. We call this the strategy trap, which is the inherent danger that comes with overemphasizing strategy and advising strategically that you actually distance yourself from your goal. The result is that others in the organization begin to think: "The communication team is only good for planning," "Our communications are just a lot of blah blah," or "I'm better off doing it myself." Obviously, that should not be your goal. After all, the business is not really interested in the strategy as such ("the planning function") but in how it will be put into practice and how it will be linked to the organization's ambitions, that is, in how it will serve the organization. Strategic competences are certainly necessary and have real value, but strategizing should never be an end in itself. The important thing is the impact your strategy achieves and the actual value it adds. Strategy, in other words, is about doing the right things the right way.

MAKING THE RIGHT CHOICES

Doing the right things the right way means you have to know what you want to achieve, what is at stake, the full range of factors to be taken into account, and what your priorities are. This is all part of your strategy. Developing a good strategy is no piece of cake. Mostly, that's because you have to make choices. And making choices is hard—ask anyone. But making choices is also unavoidable, because resources and time are always on limited supply. Statistics show that, on the whole, professionals achieve 80% of their targets by 20% of their actions (this is known as the Pareto principle). Consequently, the question to be answered is what you are doing and why, and whether you are using your time effectively.

The Communication Strategy Framework and its eight building blocks force you to make those all-important choices and provide guidance on what they should be about. That way, you can be certain to make the right choices.

COMMUNICATION STRATEGY IS AN INTEGRAL PART OF ANY PRACTITIONER'S TOOLKIT FOR SUCCESS

PAUL A. ARGENTI **ON COMMUNICATION STRATEGY**

COMMUNICATION STRATEGY

STRATEGIC COMMUNICATION IS COMMUNICATION INEXTRICABLY LINKED TO THE OVERALL STRATEGY OF AN ORGANIZATION. AS A RESULT, AN ORGANIZATION MUST HAVE A CLEAR ENOUGH STRATEGY FOR COMMUNICATORS TO WORK FROM TO HELP EXECUTE THAT STRATEGY. AND, AS MOST SENIOR EXECUTIVES HAVE SAID, YOU CANNOT EXECUTE STRATEGY IF YOU CANNOT COMMUNICATE IT IN THE FIRST PLACE.

THIS STRATEGIC APPROACH TO COMMUNICATION REQUIRES YOU TO LOOK AT COMMUNICATION FROM THE PERSPECTIVE OF YOUR AUDIENCE AND ANSWER THE QUESTION: "AS A RESULT OF THIS COMMUNICATION, MY AUDIENCE WILL…." UNDERSTANDING WHO THAT AUDIENCE IS, WHAT THEY KNOW ABOUT THE TOPIC YOU ARE DISCUSSING, AND WHAT THEY THINK ABOUT THE ORGANIZATION IS ALSO CRITICAL TO THE SUCCESS OF THE MESSAGE. AND, THAT MESSAGE CAN BE COMMUNICATED DIRECTLY OR INDIRECTLY DEPENDING UPON HOW SENSITIVE IT IS. CHANNEL CHOICE IS SIMILARLY A STRATEGIC CHOICE AND MUST BE PICKED BASED ON WHAT IS EASIEST FOR THE AUDIENCE RATHER THAN THE COMMUNICATOR.

FINALLY, TO MEASURE SUCCESS, WE MUST ASK OURSELVES, DID THEY DO WHAT WE WANTED THEM TO DO? THIS WILL TELL US WHETHER WE ACHIEVED OUR COMMUNICATION OBJECTIVE. IN THE END, THIS ITERATIVE PROCESS OF COMMUNICATION IS WHAT WE CALL COMMUNICATION STRATEGY: AN INTEGRAL PART OF ANY PRACTITIONER'S TOOLKIT FOR SUCCESS.

Paul A. Argenti
Professor of Corporate Communication
The Tuck School of Business at Dartmouth College, Hanover, NH,
United States of America

THIS IS STRATEGY

Strategy is a term that gets used in lots of different ways. All those definitions are valid, but they can also give rise to confusion. That's because we seldom explain what we mean.

We use the term "strategy" to indicate when we have discovered a smart way to do things, or that we are thinking in terms of ends rather than means, when we are tying in with the organization's strategic roadmap, or that we are thinking about long-term payoffs instead of quick wins. These are all very different definitions, which is rather confusing.

Strategy stems from the Greek word that means, literally, "to build [agein] a road [stratos]." But originally it was also used to refer to a person who was "in command," or "to achieve through a clever ploy." Even back in ancient Greece, a strategist was equal parts architect, captain, and savvy implementer. Now the latter is something we also refer to as tactics, to distinguish it from operational implementation. That lets us pare strategy down to a function of thinking about goals. Strategy, then, means thinking about how to get to a given point and all the things you need to consider en route. This is the definition of strategy we apply here, though recognizing that the proof of a good strategy is in the application, and that it has to be continually adjusted along the way. It is also worth stating that we don't believe communication allows for divisions between thinking and doing, but we won't get into that here.

STRATEGY MEANS THINKING ABOUT HOW TO GET TO A GIVEN POINT AND ALL THE THINGS YOU NEED TO CONSIDER EN ROUTE

STRATEGY IS A COLLABORATIVE EFFORT

Strategies can never be devised in isolation. If you do not consider and involve the wider playing field, your strategy will ultimately be worthless. The Communication Strategy Framework prevents you from winding up in that dead end, because our method stresses the context in which communication takes place. A communication strategy always has to be linked to the organization's wider strategic choices and it has to make sense to everyone involved. Strategy has to be a collaborative effort.

With the Framework as your guide, you can easily demonstrate that your communication department is not a sideline activity or niche outfit that doesn't talk the management lingo, but a vital mechanism that contributes to the organization. You can also use it to make it easy to discuss your strategic considerations and choices with others in the organization or with your clients. No need for them to take a crash course or delve into the details—because the Communication Strategy Framework is not about details. It is about the essence.

MINTZBERG ON STRATEGY

Lengthy books have been written on the subject of how to think and act strategically, but the real strategy bible is Henry Mintzberg, Bruce Ahlstrand, and Joseph Lampel's *Strategy Safari* (2005). The crux of their argument is that there are multitude of visions on how to develop strategy, each with its own pros and cons, gaps and interesting perspectives. The important thing, they conclude, is to eliminate all possible drawbacks by combining various visions.

DIFFERENT CONCEPTIONS OF STRATEGY

Strategy is a word that is used in very different ways, but often without any explication. Many of these meanings have always been inherent to the concept of strategy, and by extension to that of "strategic action." In other words, strategy is a multivalent concept. We have seen it applied in at least five ways. These differences in meaning can be illustrated using the following oppositions.

Strategy as:

Intelligent move	*versus*	Reckless move
Targeted action	*versus*	Acting without considering the aims
Fits with the organizational strategy	*versus*	Unrelated to the organizational strategy
Focused on the long term	*versus*	Focused on the short term
Clear choices	*versus*	A bit of everything

Henry Mintzberg, James Brian Quinn, and Sumantra Ghoshal (2013) explain that one good way to do this is to approach strategy not as a lone but rather a collaborative process. Here they refer to the classic Indian poem about the blind men and the elephant. If you don't know this story, take a moment to Google it. The moral of the story is that one person can only ever perceive a small piece of reality. That's how it is with communication strategy too. When you design your strategy in isolation, confined by your own reality, you can easily miss seeing the reality of other parts of the organization.

STRATEGY IS DYNAMIC

In 1985 Henry Mintzberg and James A. Waters published a paper in the Strategic Management Journal setting out their vision on the strategy process. They distinguished between the intended, deliberate, emergent, and realized strategy. The intended strategy is what you initially decided to do. The deliberate strategy is the part of the intended strategy that you actually pursue. The emergent strategy is what evolves along the way as you contend with developments that you could not have foreseen beforehand. The realized strategy is the sum of the deliberate and the emergent strategy. Basically, what you decide to do beforehand will not necessarily match up with what you accomplish in the end. This idea was the inspiration for the Communication Strategy Framework.

Figure 2. The Mintzberg and Waters Strategy Model

What you ultimately accomplish therefore is not automatically what you originally planned. We believe this is an incredibly important insight on the strategy process because it encapsulates so well the inherent dynamics of strategy development and implementation. The interesting thing about this approach is that even though you set a final target and map out how to get there, you also stay flexible because you factor in unexpected developments along the way. You can always adjust course. In a fast-moving environment, companies need to accelerate change by making annual planning processes lighter and more frequent and sometimes by making episodic processes continual, say Martin Reeves and Mike Deimler (2011) in their article "Adaptability: The New Competitive Advantage."

STRATEGY DEPENDS ON CONTEXT

The strategy process can be more or less intensive, depending on the variables of the context. Choices have to stay up for discussion because the situation changes, the organizational mission changes, or because you find that the choices you made simply were not as targeted as they needed to be. The Communication Strategy Framework helps you to identify where you want to go, everything you have to consider along the way, and who and what you expect to need to reach your goal.

We like to compare the Communication Strategy Framework to planning a sailing trip. Before you set out, you plot a course. En route, you have to make constant adjustments—due to the changing wind, countercurrents, because you are taking the waves at the wrong angle and that's uncomfortable, or because you are on a collision course and likely will have to give way. There are even times that you have to change your destination mid-trip because you realize that it is no longer viable or where you need to go. So too you have to adjust your ambitions. It may feel like failure, but it shouldn't. In actuality, recalibrating takes smart, strategic thinking. And the big advantage is that it keeps you relevant. A watertight action plan is precisely what you do not want. Broad strokes are enough; the details will fill themselves in after you get started, in the course of your journey.

STRATEGY IS A PERMANENT PRIORITY

The Communication Strategy Framework is a method for reaching agreement on what really matters, the factors to be considered, and what is needed to bring about those things that matter. As well as gathering as much input as possible, this also requires you to periodically discuss alternately fundamental and more pragmatic aspects with each other, in a process of continuous reflection. Not by meeting in boardrooms, but by pausing and stepping back to look at what you are doing and what you should be doing. This combination of rational and creative thinking is also known as heuristics—the art of discovery—and works best when you invest the time to explore, have fun with it, and do that together.

[**Heuristics**]

• *As in "eureka!" from the Greek heurèka, meaning "I've found it!"*

Heuristics is the science, theory, or art of discovery, the aim of which is to invent or discover by methodical and systematic means.

But it doesn't stop there. Having made choices, you have to keep revisiting them along the way. Strategy requires ongoing maintenance. Ideally, we recommend that before every key meeting or decision time, everyone examines whether any choices made in the Framework need revision. Evaluating how far earlier versions of the Communication Strategy Framework are still adequate and making adjustments if not has to be a permanent priority. In short, you have to be equal parts architect, captain, and a savvy tactician all in one. Which is precisely our definition of a good strategist.

WHEN DO YOU
NEED A STRATEGY?

- Your organization is planning an extensive change program. Besides an efficiency boost, the aim is to put customers top of mind again organization-wide. The communication department is asked to design a strategy that will contribute to achieving the program goals.

- A new CEO or director is appointed who wants to overhaul everything. Every department has to submit a new plan to align with the new course. The communication department is asked to develop a strategy to guide the new executive's successful entry into the organization.

- Your organization has a fixed planning cycle that calls for everyone to deliver their plans at set times. In summer you start formulating priorities for next year. What is the status of previous strategic choices? Are they still valid?

- A crisis has put a big dent in trust in the organization and its reputation has suffered. What will you do in the next twelve months to restore trust among employees, clients, customers, and stakeholders?

- Your organization has acquired a competitor. The communication department is asked to develop a communication strategy to aid their integration in your organization.

YOU MAKE STRATEGIC CHOICES ALL THE TIME, OFTEN WITHOUT EVEN BEING AWARE OF IT. AND THAT'S OKAY, BUT SOMETIMES YOU NEED TO AMPLIFY THE STRATEGY PROCESS. WHEN? AND WHY? HERE ARE SOME SITUATIONS WHERE STRATEGY IS CRUCIAL.

- Your organization's core product has come under fire. NGOs and stakeholders are threatening to cut your license to operate. How should the communication department respond?

- You are hired as a consultant to tackle some specific issues. To get started, you have to furnish a vision setting out your plan of action. What is the main thrust of your plan? What is the long-term goal?

- The CEO asks you into her office. She tells you about a merger in the pipeline and asks you to coordinate communication around the acquisition. Now you have to come up with a strategy.

Of course, we are all strategizing all the time, in the sense of trying to make smart moves—from deciding on an opener for your pitch to the tone you take in a conversation, and from the images you choose to illustrate a presentation to the way you advise a client or the interventions you select to solve a communication issue. Done right, strategic actions are the combined product of your personal choices and experiences and the overarching aims you define with one another. That is where the Communication Strategy Framework comes in.

THE COMMUNICATION STRATEGY FRAMEWORK

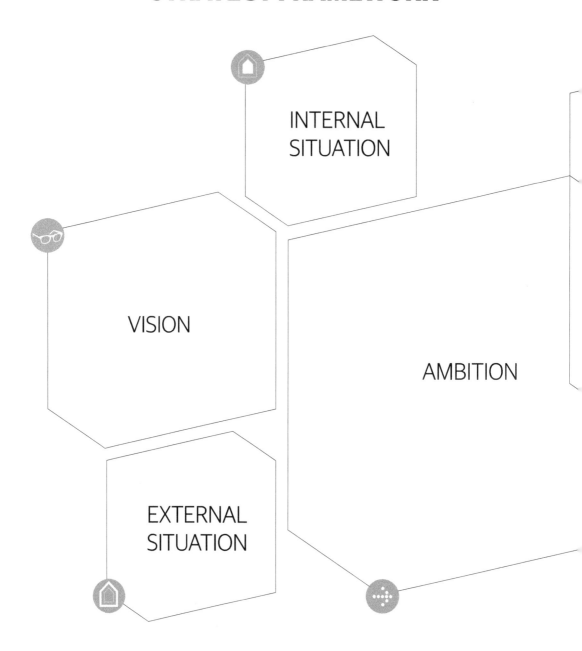

Figure 3. The Communication Strategy Framework (copyright Betteke van Ruler and Frank Körver)

STAKEHOLDERS

ACCOUNTABILITY

GAME PLAN

RESOURCES

THE COMMUNICATION STRATEGY FRAMEWORK HELPS YOU TO MAKE CHOICES

The Communication Strategy Framework helps you to make strategic choices. Your goal is to make choices concise enough to fit on a single sheet of paper or slide, rather than writing a long rambling plan that ends up merely collecting dust on the shelf. The advantage is that this forces you to keep it simple and straightforward (KISS), to be clear in your formulations and stick to essentials, but also—and more importantly—clearly shows if your choices are congruent with each other. Say you conclude that the internal situation outweighs the externals, then your ambitions will accordingly have to target internal factors, and you will likely need to ally with HR. If your strategy involves changing the behavior of certain target publics, then besides the expertise of the communication department, you will also need to draw on other organizational divisions, or other organizations altogether. After all, behavior changes are rarely achieved through communication alone; you need to deploy a broad front.

TIME EQUALS QUALITY

Over the years, we have sought out and applied inventive methods to arrive at strategic choices. In the process we noticed that if you can manage to sum up your strategy on a single sheet on paper, you have won half the battle.

However, don't make the mistake of thinking this is faster than writing a 20-page plan. Working with the Communication Strategy Framework requires a significant time and energy investment. In the first place, to make choices, then to discuss those choices with others, and finally to make them as clear-cut as possible. This takes real time, but you also have to build in margins to allow choices and their implications to sink in. Take a tip from the old adage and "sleep on it." After all, the choices you make will largely define communication in and about the organization and the impact that communication achieves.

Giving yourself enough time—demanding it if necessary—is no luxury, and will pay off with visible results once you know how to apply the Communication Strategy Framework successfully. You will be able to show all your stakeholders what choices you have made and what actions.

THE COMMUNICATION STRATEGY FRAMEWORK CONSISTS OF EIGHT BUILDING BLOCKS THAT TOGETHER SHOW THE CHOICES YOU MAKE, WHAT YOUR GOAL IS, WHAT AND WHO YOU NEED TO ACHIEVE IT, AND WHERE YOUR PRIORITIES LIE. THE FRAMEWORK THUS GIVES YOU INSTANT INSIGHT INTO WHAT YOU ARE AND ARE NOT DOING AND, JUST AS IMPORTANTLY, WHY.

1 The Communication Strategy Framework is a practical guide to use in the strategy development process.

2 The Communication Strategy Framework helps you to enlarge your professional impact by linking content with process.

3 The Communication Strategy Framework helps you make fundamental and rational strategic choices.

4 The Communication Strategy Framework transparently maps out your accountabilities.

5 The Communication Strategy Framework provides a foundation for all your actions, functioning as a compass and touchstone for daily work.

6 The Communication Strategy Framework helps you to find and sustain focus.

ORIENTATION AND IMPLEMENTATION

The Communication Strategy Framework is divided into two halves: left and right. The left half helps you choose your orientation, the right half is focused on implementation. As you progress through your implementation, you will continue to revisit the left half and reevaluate. What choices did you start out with? Are they really realistic? Are there implementation issues that you can foresee from the outset? Excellent! The Communication Strategy Framework is an iterative model. Choices you make in one building block impact on the choices you make in the others. For this reason, the building blocks are not numbered; that could imply they are a series of steps to cross off. They're not. To some extent there is a sequence: you cannot formulate an ambition, for example, without first articulating your vision on the role of communication and analyzing the internal and external situations; however, different building blocks can be tackled simultaneously. Also, you have to routinely check and recheck whether your choices remain congruent with each other, as only then will your whole strategy actually cohere.

DO YOU NEED THE COMMUNICATION STRATEGY FRAMEWORK?

ON THE RIGHT ARE TEN STATEMENTS
Give yourself 1 point for each statement you agree with, and 0 points for those you disagree with. Total your points and then check your score.

Scored 0 points?
Stop reading. You don't need the Communication Strategy Framework. Give it to someone who does.

Scored between 1 and 5 points?
Congratulations, you are well on your way, and with a little extra nudge will achieve great heights.

Scored more than 5 points?
Excellent, you are exactly the person we wrote this book for. Now it's time to get to work!

DOES COMMUNICATION STRATEGY REALLY REQUIRE A METHOD? ISN'T THAT AN OUTDATED AND OVERCOMPLICATED APPROACH TO THINGS? WE CHALLENGE YOU TO TAKE THE TEST.

1 Developing plans is something I dread because it is always such a chore.
2 We have no shortage of plans, but no one knows about them.
3 We are unable to make choices. We want to do it all, so the plan keeps on growing.
4 We can't find a clear way to explain or visualize our plan.
5 We are having a hard time linking communication to our organizational priorities.
6 No one seems to really appreciate how hard we work and how much we do.
7 Whenever I discuss my plans with my boss, I run out of time.
8 Whenever I discuss my plans with my boss, we mainly talk about the budget or about the video that he wants to make and I don't.
9 When I discuss my strategy document with others, they tend to start browsing through it after a few seconds.
10 I'm unhappy with the way we have been carrying out our plans until now; it is time for a change.

THE COMMUNICATION STRATEGY FRAMEWORK

A practical method with eight building blocks

THE
COMMUNICATION
STRATEGY
FRAMEWORK
EXPLAINED

8 BUILDING BLOCKS
FOR THE COMMUNICATION
STRATEGY FRAMEWORK

BUILDING BLOCK **VISION**

A vision articulating the what, why, and how of your shared task provides direction for each person's activities. What are you a professional of? A vision helps you to explain to others exactly what that contribution is. Without an explicit vision, you will just keep traveling down the same old road. Inviting discussion of your vision is also crucial to be able to innovate. A communication professional understands how communication works and can explain it to others. They also know what's happening in their field and can contribute to internal discussions with new ideas and angles, always asking how communication should function within their own organizational context and how communication professionals can add value to that communication. A vision is not static; it evolves. These are the facets of this building block.

BUILDING BLOCK **INTERNAL SITUATION**

A coherent view of the organization's internal situation is essential to make good choices about communication strategy and its implementation. But all too often this link is missing. As a result, no one really knows what value the communication activities are adding for which internal situation. Only with a good grasp of the internal situation can you also ask critical questions about your own added value and make choices about where communication priorities should lie. This encompasses the strategic choices of other departments or general management, issues in the organization, and the internal climate among staff. But you also have to consider internal attitudes to communication. This concerns not so much the department itself but the role communication is assigned in the organization, which of course influences what is expected of you as communication professionals. That is what this building block is about.

FOR THIS BOOK WE HAVE CHOSEN TO PRESENT THE BUILDING BLOCKS IN A PAR-TICULAR SEQUENCE, WHICH YOU MAY ALSO WISH TO FOLLOW ONCE YOU START WORKING WITH THE MODEL. HOWEVER, AS YOU GO ALONG YOU WILL ROUTINELY FIND YOURSELF REVISITING EARLIER BUILDING BLOCKS TO SEE WHAT YOU DID AND WHETHER THE CHOICES YOU MADE STILL FIT THOSE YOU MAKE AT A LATER STAGE. IT CAN ALSO BE HELPFUL TO PROJECT AHEAD OCCASIONALLY AND THINK ABOUT CHOICES YOU MIGHT MAKE IN SUBSEQUENT BUILDING BLOCKS.

BUILDING BLOCK **EXTERNAL SITUATION**

These days, organizations have to be more attuned than ever to how they relate to the outside world. Mainly this concerns communication with specific publics, but also the question of how and by what means and channels the organization profiles itself externally in general. To be caught off guard by public opinion or a sentiment among stakeholders usually means it is too late to do anything about it. To do your job well, you have to know what is happening in the world outside the organization and where to target your approach. Those insights can help not only to hone your own approach, but also to underscore that you are a serious discussion **partner.** If you know what is going on in the outside world then you can contribute to better internal decision-making by sharing those insights with senior management and getting key issues prioritized. That is the focus of this building block.

BUILDING BLOCK **AMBITION**

Ambition is the pursuit of a particular objective, but it is also the objective itself—the destination you ultimately hope to reach. Ambition is also bound up with the idea of being committed to something and craving success. Ambition as we define it here is the product of the building blocks of Vision, Internal Situation, and External Situation. Not in the form of an equation, but as targeted choices. This building block centers on two key questions: What is your core mission, and what are your core values? Or, put differently, what do you stand for and what motivates you? What do you aspire to accomplish and what core values does your communication need to harness to do so? Ambition determines your orientation and expresses the purpose and the added value of the communication field in the current situation. You could also think of it as a qualitative target or your goals. These are the facets of this building block.

BUILDING BLOCK **ACCOUNTABILITY**

Accountability is about making your added value explicit. It is about taking responsibility and answering for your actions. The responsibilities of a communication department may seem obvious, but in practice that is not always the case. You have to make it clear what you are responsible for and how, and which responsibilities lie elsewhere. Professionals also have to account for their actions. This is the function of performance indicators, which enable you both to measure progress toward your ambition and hold you to it, serving as guideposts to help you get and stay on track. It can also be a good idea to formulate success factors for yourself: What and who will determine whether you achieve your ambitions? That is the focus of this building block.

BUILDING BLOCK **STAKEHOLDERS**

Communication is not just the responsibility of the communication department, nor can most ambitions be achieved through communication alone. Lots of people, groups, and organizations may be involved in shaping and determining—and possibly hindering—your strategy's success, starting with your target publics. But equally important are your supporters and allies. These days, you have to factor in a whole spectrum of stakeholders. The most important ones for communication strategy are, firstly, the users, then the influencers and sponsors who have to commit to the strategy or in any case be kept in loop (the enablers), and finally the partners whose active contributions are needed to achieve the communication ambitions. How you identify these stakeholders and ways of relating to them are the focus of this building block.

BUILDING BLOCK **RESOURCES**

You may have big ambitions, but you also have to be realistic. To attain what you want, you have to tap into diverse resources, not only stakeholders but also staff and money. After all, big ambitions require big resources. This should be obvious, yet there is an increasing push these days to do more with less money and less staff, and that often requires competences the organization does not have. That throws up a complex albeit interesting challenge for communication directors, and usually means you have to reconsider who is responsible for what and how (the Accountability building block). It may be that contributions from outside the communication department are needed to realize the ambition. However you tackle this, it should be evident that there is a symbiotic relationship between resources and ambition: a complex ambition cannot be accomplished with scant resources, nor a strategically oriented and complex ambition with operational staff only. That is the focus of this building block.

BUILDING BLOCK **GAME PLAN**

The Game Plan building block is the proof of the pudding: this is where everything formulated in the other building blocks comes together in targeted, strategic choices for implementation. If you are unable to make clear choices or the choices you make fail to align with the other building blocks, you will have to revisit them or else change your game plan. In business, the game plan usually takes the shape of an operational plan of action with a timeline and detailed budget. We mean something different. At this stage in our Framework, the game plan is the targeted choices you make based on the other building blocks in order to provide the orientation for your operational activities. In classical planning this is often referred to as strategy, but it is really about tactics. Two questions are central here: What is your implementation strategy, and how will you assign priorities (what will you do first, what can wait until later)? These are the considerations of this building block.

ORIENTATION: THE LEFT PART OF THE COMMUNICATION STRATEGY FRAMEWORK

A closer look at the left part of the model: Vision, Internal Situation, External Situation, and Ambition

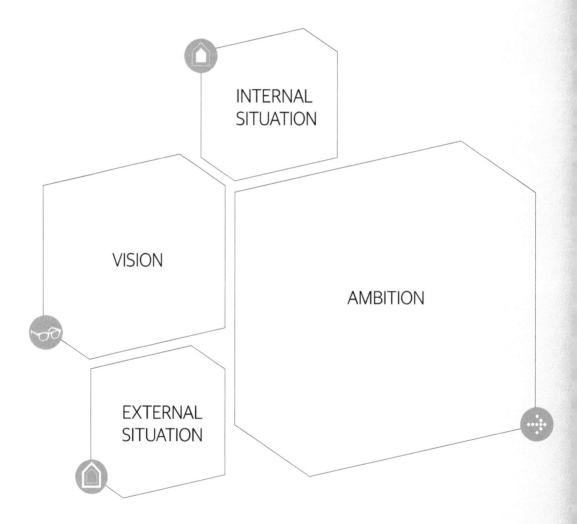

Figure 4. Left part of the Communication Strategy Framework

VISION

There are several key questions that every communication professional routinely has to ask themselves: What is good communication? What role should communication play in our organization? How do we define our role and added value in that communication? What is my own vision on this? And what can the organization expect us to deliver?

INTERNAL SITUATION

Understanding what is happening inside the organization and the strategic choices made in other departments is essential to make the right strategy choices about communication. Without that coherence, it will be impossible to explain your strategy's value. This building block helps you to pose critical questions about the internal situation as seen through your particular vision on communication.

EXTERNAL SITUATION

Most organizations operate in quite a turbulent playing field. To excel as a communication expert, you have to understand the game, the players, and the arena in which it is being played, and be able to interpret it from a communication angle. Rather than collecting all the data, the trick is to distinguish what is crucial for your own organization and its communications.

AMBITION

An ambition is a statement of what you want to accomplish. Firstly, it is framed by the set of core values that are paramount in the given situation, thus crystallizing which conditions your communication has to meet. Secondly, it sets out your expert opinion on what the organization's communication goals should be. Bear in mind, however, that this is not necessarily the same as your tasks as a department, since the implementation may involve or be carried out by others as well.

BUILDING BLOCK
VISION

More than twenty years ago Jim Collins and Jerry I. Porras (1996/2011) stressed the importance of vision. "The rare ability to manage continuity and change—requiring a consciously practiced discipline—is closely linked to the ability to develop a vision. Vision provides guidance about what to preserve and what to change" (2011, p. 78). Vision directs and gives meaning to what you do and how you do it. It articulates how you see something—in this case, communication and the role of the comms department. A good vision paints a picture that is inspiring and compelling for others. It also lets you stand back from the hype and objectively assess events.

A communication department with a vision demonstrates responsibility and leadership. According to management guru John Naisbitt, "Strategic planning is worthless—unless there is first a strategic vision" ("John Naisbitt Quotes," n.d.). The cornerstone of a sound strategy is a clear vision. That is why the first building block of the Communication Strategy Framework is vision. We believe that a good vision has a positive effect on efficiency and efficacy. What leaders do well, said John Adair (2009), the pioneer on leadership, is inspire others to complete a common task. However, he added, that is only possible if there is a vision on what that common task is and why it is impor-tant. Developing and promoting a vision is therefore essential. It shows that you take your work seriously, have a sense of what the organization needs, and want to take charge.

As well as providing a compass, your vision is also a touchstone. It determines how your department—and you as a director, advisor, or officer—are judged by the rest of the organization. You have to stay focused: Why are we doing what we're doing? How will it benefit the organization? And then continue honing your vision along the way.

EVERY COMMUNICATION DEPARTMENT SHOULD ROUTINELY ASK ITSELF THESE
VITAL QUESTIONS: WHAT ARE OUR ROLE AND OUR ADDED VALUE IN THE ORGANI-
ZATION NOW, AND WHAT SHOULD THEY BE? WHAT DO WE TAKE RESPONSIBILITY
FOR, AND WHAT CAN THE ORGANIZATION EXPECT US TO DELIVER?

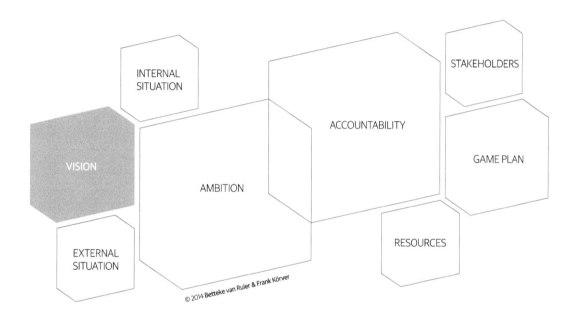

© 2014 Betteke van Ruler & Frank Körver

**TO DEVELOP OR REFINE A VISION, YOU NEED TO ANSWER
TWO QUESTIONS:**

1   What developments are occurring in the communication field and which
    ones are relevant to us?
2   What tangible contribution can communication make to achieving the
    organization's objectives, and what is the communication professional's
    role in that contribution?

⌐ Beware!
   *Developing a vision is easier said than done. The danger is that it proves
   to be merely a paper tiger, implausible, or fundamentally unsuited to the
   organization's needs. A vision never exists in a vacuum; rather, it offers a
   lens through which to look at the internal and external situations.*

5 KICKSTARTERS

1   WHAT DO YOU VIEW TO BE THE UNIQUE POWER OF COMMUNICATION?

2   WHAT THREE DEVELOPMENTS IN THE COMMUNICATION FIELD WILL MOST IMPACT YOUR ORGANIZATION IN THE YEARS AHEAD?

3   WHAT THREE DEVELOPMENTS IN THE COMMUNICATION FIELD WILL MOST IMPACT YOUR COMMUNICATION DEPARTMENT?

4   HOW CAN A COMMUNICATION DEPARTMENT MAKE THE DIFFERENCE, AND WHAT WOULD THE ORGANIZATION LACK WITHOUT IT?

5   HOW DOES YOUR DEPARTMENT OR TEAM WANT TO BE REGARDED AND RECOGNIZED BY THE REST OF THE ORGANIZATION AND MANAGEMENT?

VISION ON THE FIELD OF COMMUNICATION

Communication as a field is continually evolving. A communication professional can be expected to have a thorough grasp of developments and an opinion on how those developments impact the organization's communication policy. A sound vision shows that you understand how communication works and how it can be leveraged by a communication professional—in essence, that you understand the fundamentals of your field—but equally that you are attuned to the times, the issues relevant to stakeholders and society at large, and can package that in a relevant way. It also shows that you can translate what the developments in the communication field mean for your organization. For instance, you understand how social media will impact conceptions of good communication and that the ubiquity of tablets and smartphones have made the principle of "anywhere, any time, any device" more relevant than ever, as well as the repercussions that fake news can have on your organization's reputation.

Excellent communication is implemented by excellent communication professionals, say Ralph Tench and his co-authors Dejan Verčič, Ansgar Zerfass, Angeles Moreno, and Piet Verhoeven in the ten-year study *Communication Excellence: How to Develop, Manage and Lead Exceptional Communications* (2016); "Excellent communication professionals are sagacious, linked and solid." Sagacious professionals are knowledgeable, demonstrating reflective wisdom as well as shrewdness and at times applying appropriate mental discernment. Linked professionals are personally and professionally networked individuals who understand the importance of collaboration with colleagues through mentoring and mentorship. Solid professionals show a solidity driven by personal, organizational and professional ethics and frameworks (p. 135).

A VISION GIVES YOU A HEAD START

One of the big challenges now is that communication is increasingly seen as something everybody in the organization can do. Social media have afforded all employees the tools to present their projects to the world, even to make the news, enabling more people than ever before—from the receptionist to the CEO—to form an opinion about the merits and missteps of communication. Of course, we can question whether communication was ever really the sole preserve of communication professionals; however, the direction of social media paired with growing reputation awareness raises fundamental questions about what communication is and is not, and to what extent communication can and ought to be managed.

A CLEAR VISION IS KISS-ABLE

Developing a clear vision is hard work, so take the time to do it right.
Your vision should express what solid communication means in and for your
organization and how it is effectuated by the communication professional.

The following questions will help you to formulate your vision:

1   Good communication is already crucial for [organization name] because…
    (Don't forget to make explicit what you mean by "good" communication)

2   The role of communication will become ever more important for
    [organization name] in the years ahead because…

3   Our communication team/I, as a communication professional, will play
    a key role in that communication because we/I…

A solid vision also needs to be KISS-able: Keep It Simple and Straightforward.
Make your vision as crystal clear as possible. That will make it easier for you
to remember and for others to understand.

Precisely these factors make it more important than ever to have a clear vision
on communication and the role of the communication professional within it,
and to articulate that vision. In cultivating your expertise, we believe it is crucial
to always stay one step ahead of the organization. That will cement your position as a serious discussion partner and authority on communication and help
to fuel innovation.

TREND STUDIES CAN BE USEFUL
An explicit vision is the product of a reflective and, ideally, collaborative process. Trend studies can be a good source of input for this process, helping to
pinpoint what is relevant in your situation, matters on which you have to take
a stance, and fronts on which you need to innovate. Trend studies can spark
dialogue about a broader spectrum of issues and help you decide which ones
matter to your department, organization, and clients.

New studies are being published all the time—many also on the Internet—on every aspect of communication, as well as on relevant developments in related fields like technology, organizational science, and sociology, and spanning trends from the local to the global level.

THE ADDED VALUE OF A COMMUNICATION DEPARTMENT

An important question that every communication department should periodically ask itself is: What role can we and do we want to play in our organization? What do you, as professionals, take responsibility for and what can the organization expect you to deliver? This question is equally valid for agencies and their clients. Oddly enough, we have found that many communication professionals have trouble articulating this.

Essentially, it is about your positioning and proposition. Positioning is the specific, unique role you choose to fulfill in or for an organization; a role that is deemed useful in that organization and that no one else fulfills. Your proposition, which follows on from your position, is your core promise. What can you do for the organization? A fresh way to come at this question that primes you to think about what matters is to brainstorm what the organization would lack if it had no communication department or agency at all.

Often departments find themselves with severely reduced budgets yet expectations that are as high or higher than ever. That makes it crucial to keep asking: What is our actual task and which core qualities and core values does it require? Never let others answer these questions for you. It is better for you to define the answers yourself, because that leaves you in control. Think and talk about this routinely as a team and have the courage to take a stand. And, of course, get the management to commit as well.

Developing your own vision is important, so do it carefully. The choices you make now will define how your department evolves in the years ahead. How should you structure the team? What core competences do you need? How will you allocate resources? Who do you need as allies? Making choices is unavoidable. You cannot do everything, after all, and otherwise someone else will just wind up choosing for you. Scenario planning, which automatically crystallizes your options, offers a fun way to tackle those choices.

THE 4 C'S OF COMMUNICATION

COUNSELING

Counseling focuses on the analysis of changes in public sentiment, meaning the views held on issues by society at large and especially by key stakeholders, and internal discussions about the organization's own views on issues, which impact on its operations and overall policy. Catchwords here are monitoring, analysis, and corporate identity. The communication professional acts as a counselor or sparring partner on the internal style of the house.

COACHING

Coaching is about assisting the individuals in the organization with their communications, as directed by the organization's strategic choices and viewpoints and corporate identity. This subfield, therefore, builds on principles identified through counseling. Coaching and the role of the coach or facilitator is focused on education, training, and process advice, and centers on the coworkers in the organization.

CONCEPTUALIZATION

The third subfield is about developing sound communication programs as a means to gain and maintain understanding, trust, positive ties, or a good reputation. Insofar as it is about implementing the organization's mission and policy, it too builds on the counseling component, and is concerned with targets, organizational capacity, knowledge of what could and probably will not work (educated guessing), and research and planning proficiency. Increasingly, this subfield is using agile methods such as scrum.

CREATION

The classic domain of communication professionals is the production of means of communication. Catchwords are creativity, knowledge of tools, and a focus on customers (both the client and the target group). Communication professionals in this subfield are sometimes disparaged as just churning out messages, but nothing is more strategic than crafting the right opening sentence. Creation is where the effects of counseling, coaching, and conceptualization come to fruition.

From:
Betteke van Ruler, 2012

THE TYPICAL TASKS OF COMMUNICATION DEPARTMENTS
There are many national and international studies into the role of the communication department. A survey conducted some years ago among scholars and teachers
in twenty-four European countries identified four subfields of the communication
profession: counseling, coaching, conceptualization, and creation (van Ruler and
Verčič, 2008, see also van Ruler, 2012). Conceptualization and creation have been
recognized as part of the field from the beginning, but the other two were entirely
new at the time.

That all four are commonly accepted nowadays is also attested in Communication
Excellence, which reviews a decade of European Communication Monitors. In their
ten-year study, Tench et al. (2016) conclude that European communication departments now have three fields of activity: first, a performance function focused
on activities such as listening to stakeholders, writing messages, and organizing
events. Second, a management function, where such activities are disposed and
aligned. Third, a so-called second-order management function, which influences
the management behavior of top executives and their peers by confronting them
with public opinion, critical issues, and alternative views about the organization.

> "In a typical week, communicators spend more than one-third of their produc-
> tive time at work for operational communication (e.g. talking to colleagues and
> media, writing texts, monitoring and organising events). Managing activities
> related to planning, organising, leading staff, evaluating strategies, justifying
> spending and preparing for crises takes also about one-third of their time.
> Almost 20 per cent of the time is used for reflective communication manage-
> ment like aligning communication between the organisation and its stakehol-
> ders. Coaching, training and enabling members of the organisation or (internal)
> clients take almost 20 per cent as well. The latter area has risen slightly over the
> years, which has suggested that coaching has become more important." (Tench
> et al., 2016, pp. 118–119)

A Dutch survey on the roles of communication departments demonstrated that
while reputation is considered one of the vital functions of communication departments, respondents (communication directors) simultaneously regard this to be
a rather limited view of their role (Körver, 2012). Communication, they feel, ought
to play a central role in propelling internal change, connecting inside and outside
world, and facilitating managers to communicate more effectively. Discussing the
outcomes of this survey with communication directors and practicing with the four
roles during work sessions revealed a growing demand for departments that also
provide input on the organization's primary processes, effectively assuming the fifth
role of a business partner, which was added in 2016.

THE 5 ROLES OF A COMMUNICATION DEPARTMENT

Brand leader

The brand leader spearheads the brand and reputation and assumes the task of creating a distinctive brand and strong reputation. The brand is the cornerstone of everything the organization does and plays a decisive role in the battle to win public favor.

Change accelerator

The change accelerator inspires and guides organizations to evolve. Organizations have to respond to a society that is changing at an unprecedented fast pace. Communication helps organizations to be more agile.

Enabler

The enabler facilitates, advises, and coaches managers and other key actors in the organization. Everyone in the organization communicates, and communication helps management to optimally fulfill its communicative tasks.

Linking pin

The linking pin connects the internal and external worlds (insofar as that distinction still exists). Organizations have to secure a foothold in the public arena. The linking pin is conversant with current issues and uses this insight to ensure the organization acts effectively.

Business partner

The business partner supports the organization in realizing primarily commercial goals. Their focus is much more on customers and market position. Communication contributes to improving customer perceptions and reinforces the primary process.

These role descriptions can aid you in determining what your department should focus on. It goes without saying that these roles are by no means set in stone, but they can help you along in formulating a vision.

⌐ From:

personal evaluations,

Frank Körver, 2016

10 DO'S AND DON'TS

1   Do think big and outside the box. You can always make concessions at a later stage.

2   Don't think in terms of limitations, but in opportunities. Strive to inspire.

3   Do use the organization's ambitions, strategy, and priorities as a jumping off point.

4   Do draw on developments in your field and your own communication knowledge as secondary input.

5   Don't involve only senior staff in the development process but specifically also include younger talents with fresh insights. This often yields surprising outcomes and enhances departmental engagement and acceptance.

6   Do put your vision on paper; this will push you to make choices. Also take the time to discuss the end product with the coworkers in your department at various stages. And do show your enthusiasm!

7   Do get management on board. Know their concerns, link them to the process, and get their input about the outcomes. If possible, also give them active roles in the development process.

8   Don't use jargon. A solid vision is written in plain language and is engaging to read. Nothing will alienate readers faster than incomprehensible technical jargon and vague formulations.

9   Do harness the power of imagery and symbolism. Engaging a creative in the process can often work wonders.

10 Do use your vision as a compass and a touchstone, and revisit it regularly to be sure it stays meaningful and current.

THIS BUILDING BLOCK IS ABOUT VISION. WITHOUT AN EXPLICIT VISION, YOU WILL SIMPLY CONTINUE DOING WHAT YOU HAVE ALWAYS DONE. BY MAKING YOUR VISION EXPLICIT, YOU CAN START TO THINK ABOUT HOW RELEVANT AND/OR VALID IT IS, WHAT YOU NEED TO ADJUST, AND HOW. HAVING A VISION HELPS YOU TO INNOVATE. A SOLID VISION INCORPORATES RELEVANT ORGANIZATIONAL DEVELOPMENTS IN COMMUNICATION PRACTICE AND SHOWS THAT YOU HAVE MADE CHOICES ABOUT THE ROLE YOU WANT TO PLAY.

IT IS MORE IMPORTANT TO DO THE RIGHT THING THAN TO DO THINGS RIGHT

COMMUNICATION STRATEGY

IT IS WIDELY RECOGNIZED THAT COMMUNICATION PROFESSIONALS WORK AS COMMUNICATION TECHNICIANS IN MANY DAY TO DAY ACTIVITIES, SUCH AS WRITING, COORDINATING PRODUCTION OF MATERIALS, ARRANGING EVENTS, AND SO ON. BUT IT IS EQUALLY OR EVEN MORE IMPORTANT THAT THEY ARE CAPABLE COMMUNICATION STRATEGISTS. AS PETER DRUCKER SAID: "IT IS MORE IMPORTANT TO DO THE RIGHT THING THAN TO DO THINGS RIGHT".

OF COURSE IT IS IMPORTANT TO DO THINGS RIGHT BY HAVING THE RE-QUIRED TECHNICAL SKILLS, BUT WHAT DRUCKER WAS POINTING OUT IS THAT THERE IS NO VALUE IN DOING THINGS WELL IF YOU ARE DOING THE WRONG THINGS. IDENTIFYING THE RIGHT THINGS TO DO IS THE ROLE OF STRATEGIC PLANNING AND STRATEGY.

TO ACHIEVE DESIRED OUTCOMES AND IMPACT, NOT JUST PRODUCE OUT-PUTS, COMMUNICATION PROFESSIONALS NEED TO BE ABLE TO BUILD EVIDENCE-BASED STRATEGY USING TOOLS SUCH AS AUDIENCE RESEARCH AND STRATEGIC PLANNING MODELS.

Jim Macnamara, Ph.D.
Distinguished Professor of Public Communication
University of Technology, Sydney, Australia

BUILDING BLOCK
INTERNAL SITUATION

Most plans start out with an analysis of the outside world. An analysis of the internal situation may follow, or it may not. We see both as being equally important, but think it makes more sense to start with an internal analysis for the following reason. Not everything happening in the world outside is important. The focus should be on matters that affect or could impact the organization, however, it is impossible to know what those matters are until you know and understand the internal situation. Moreover, if you start with what is happening in your surroundings, you run the risk of seeing your internal situation as a limitation; as something that impedes you. This is why the Communication Strategy Framework tackles the internal situation before the external situation. However, since the Framework is designed on an iterative model with building blocks that interact, it is very possible that the subsequent analysis of the external situation may lead you to adjust your focus on the internal situation.

Knowing and understanding your own organization may sound like a straightforward exercise, but in most cases, it's not. The challenge lies in prioritizing and interpreting your information. What are the main organizational ambitions and challenges in which communication can play an active part? What keeps senior management awake at night? What are staff talking about? What are key communication-related concerns in the business units? Does middle management understand and support the organization's strategic roadmap? What is the organization's communication style? How do people within the organization view communication and the communication department's activities? When working out a communication strategy, these are some of the questions you should be discussing routinely.

UNDERSTANDING WHAT IS HAPPENING INSIDE THE ORGANIZATION IS ESSENTIAL TO MAKING THE RIGHT STRATEGIC CHOICES FOR YOUR COMMUNICATION. WITHOUT THAT CONNECTION, IT WILL BE IMPOSSIBLE TO EXPLAIN YOUR STRATEGY'S VALUE.

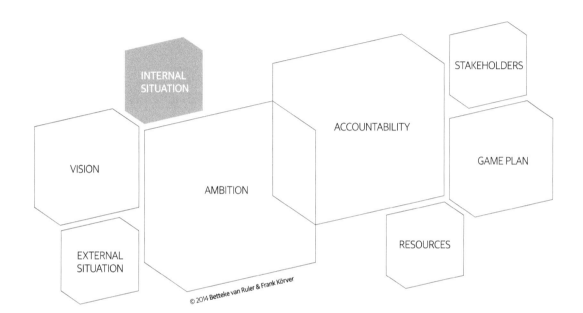

© 2014 Betteke van Ruler & Frank Körver

WHEN MAPPING OUT THE INTERNAL SITUATION, TWO QUESTIONS ARE PARAMOUNT:

1 What is happening inside our organization?
2 What is our organization's characteristic communication style?

◤ Beware!
The crux of this building block is to distill what is genuinely relevant from all the information available to you and to focus on that. Use the 80-20 Pareto princi-ple: 20% of the data determines 80 percent of the results. So, what is that 20%? Unfortunately, there is no rule for that. You'll have to figure it out together.

5 KICKSTARTERS

1   WHAT ARE THE ORGANIZATION'S MISSION, AMBITION, AND OBJECTIVES?

2   WHAT ARE THE MAIN PRIORITIES OF SENIOR MANAGEMENT AND WHAT ARE THE AMBITIONS OF OTHER DEPARTMENTS?

3   WHAT ARE THE MAIN COMMUNICATION ISSUES TO BE RESOLVED, ACCORDING TO SENIOR MANAGEMENT? ACCORDING TO OTHER DEPARTMENTS?

4   WHAT TOPICS DOMINATE CASUAL CONVERSATION AT THE HEAD OFFICE? IN THE BUSINESS?

5   WHAT IS THE DOMINANT COMMUNICATION STYLE IN THE ORGANIZATION?

AMBITIONS AND PRIORITIES

If you want to get a sense of what is happening inside the organization, you have to know three things: the ambitions, strategic choices, and priorities of the senior management; the most important internal issues; and the organization's typical communication style.

In pursuing its mission and ambitions, every organization makes strategic choices. Some organizations formulate very definite ambitions and choices from the outset, while others are more generic, or so vague that you have to do your own investigating and interviewing to figure out what they are. In some cases they are so bogged down in jargon or obscure language that you have to more or less translate them into a comprehensible form. Yet however and to whatever extent they have been articulated, those ambitions and choices always exist, even if only as negatives, such as "We will never do X again." Sometimes you can piece together a picture from precisely those things the organization has opted not to do. Whatever the case, what you want to know is: What is the organization as a whole striving for?

Staking out a communication policy that aligns with ambitions and priorities does not equate to merely playing his master's voice. On the contrary, it is only once you understand the internal situation that you can begin to ask critical questions and make your own solid choices. Like we said before, organizations set a high bar for communication professionals. Ideally, they want communication professionals to strive for maximum impact at minimum cost. The only way you can achieve that is by being selective.

STRATEGIC CHOICES

Strategic choices are the roads an organization chooses to travel to achieve its ambition. Daimler, for example, one of the biggest producers of Mercedes and other premium cars, describes its ambitions thus: "As the inventor of the automobile, we strive to be a leader in its re-invention as well. That is why we are also refining our corporate culture to become even faster, more flexible and more innovative." Daimler does this by focusing on three pillars: "1. To grow profitably worldwide in our core business. 2. To lead with our vehicles and business models centred around the CASE topics. 3. To reflect the variety, agility and requirements of our business environment with our corporate culture."

SOME ORGANIZATIONS THAT HAVE CLEARLY ARTICULATED THEIR MISSION AND AMBITIONS

Microsoft:
To empower every person and every organization on the planet to achieve more.

Ferrari:
We build cars, symbols of Italian excellence the world over, and we do so to win on both road and track. Unique creations that fuel the Prancing Horse legend and generate a "World of Dreams and Emotions."

Pepsico:
To provide consumers around the world with delicious, affordable, convenient and complementary foods and beverages from wholesome breakfasts to healthy and fun daytime snacks and beverages to evening treats.

Lego:
Inspire and develop the builders of tomorrow.

Transamerica:
To enhance the present and future economic well-being of its clients and representatives.

Strategy is always about choices and prioritizing. Usually, the choices have far-reaching consequences, whether positive or negative. In recent years, the pressure of economic developments has led to scores of large reorganizations. Often the decisions to not do something or to terminate an activity are the toughest. That, too, is a strategic choice; a type of choice more commonly made in times of heightened cost-awareness, but equally one that is rarely spelled out in strategic documents. Nonetheless, keeping track of things the organization chooses not or no longer to invest in, to phase out or to put off, is also important, because this unquestionably also influences its communication strategy. Regardless of whether the choices are positive or negative, the important thing is that you know what they are and understand what they entail, because they will of course largely direct your work as a communication professional. If the management decides to embark on a major reorganization or to adjust course over the coming years, those changes cannot help but impact choices about the organization's communication strategy. Responding to that shows you know what is happening and will enable you to deliver added value.

THREE LEVELS OF LEARNING

Current scholarly literature differentiates between single, double, and triple loop learning. When an organization is confronted with a given problem, it can address it within the prevailing business model and the preset strategic choices. This is called single-loop learning. At times, problems spark a more fundamental discussion about the organization's business model, calling the model itself into question. This is double-loop learning, which usually leads to new strategic choices and a new ambition. In triple-loop learning, transformation is permanent and innovation a constant; the organization continually questions everything.

Communication departments can play a key role in each of these forms of learning, not necessarily by making the strategic choices (that's the job of senior management), but by supplying input that improves the quality of the choices made and by supporting discussion about those choices.

BURNING ISSUES

When communication professionals talk about issues, we tend to mean things happening in the outside world. But there are always issues inside the organization, too. Issues are topics that are controversial and on which opinions differ. In issue management, an "issue" tends to be defined as an obstacle with advocates and opponents that needs to be resolved. This is something we will discuss in more detail in the External Situation building block. Here, we look at the thorny side of internal issues, which is precisely that they tend to be so difficult to grasp.

Every organization has its own burning issues. They can be about anything from underperforming departments to clashing personalities in the management board, faulty leadership or a failing vision, what to do about receding markets, obsolete IT—you name it. Compared to external issues, however, pinpointing those inside organizations often is trickier. Mostly this is because of the culture of corporate silence that stifles talk about controversial topics.

Organizations tend to have unwritten rules about what can be discussed, and how, and what is off limits. That results in corporate silence. "Various studies show that when communicating with their managers, subordinates tend to repackage information or present it in a way that mitigates the negative connotations," explains IKEA NL Chief Communication Officer Mark Blok in his book *Breaking Corporate Silence* (2013). Corporate silence in effect paralyzes an organization's capacity to change. Therefore, the issues that everyone avoids are precisely the ones that have to be broached. Identifying and prioritizing those issues is, we feel, a job for the communication team, whereas actually talking about them is the responsibility of managers themselves, and first and foremost the CEO.

Which specific burning issues need to be addressed in the communication strategy is something that you as a team will have to decide. The one thing you should never do is avoid them, no matter how sensitive they are. But do be careful about how and in what terms you frame the discussion.

A MATTER OF STYLE

Communication departments spend a lot of time thinking about the organization's visual image in the form of their name, logo, color palettes, typography, and so forth, which are all part of what we call "corporate design." Projecting a consonant image is important, as is the feeling it evokes. However, this is a very limited definition of what matters.

Instead, we believe the emphasis should be on the intrinsic factors that define the character of the organization, starting with the inhouse style of communication. This is about how people in the organization communicate with each other and interact with the outside world. Far more important than the visual branding, formal publicity, and flag-waving, is how employees act. A famous expression of Arthur Page is that the factor that determines roughly 90% of an organization's reputation is behavior (Argenti, MacDonald, and O'Neill, 2018, p. 20). Most organizations, however, and much of the communication field too, tend to view corporate communication very narrowly as constituting mainly formal marketing and publicity.

Yet this is changing fast. Communication professionals these days also want to have a say in other factors that affect the reputation of their organization, or at least to discuss them inhouse. If a help desk operator is rude to customers on the phone, for instance, that will have a far bigger impact on their reputation than any amount of publicity campaigning or a sleek website. Little surprise, then, to see that some communication departments are now concerning themselves with things like their organization's contact center or the design of the reception area. After all, that too is communication.

WHEN STYLE TURNS INTO AN ISSUE

Whereas organizations present their desired identity in formal contexts, it is the character and style of their day-to-day conduct that reveals their authentic nature. The style of daily communication both defines and expresses the culture within an organization. Ideally, it invites opportunities. In practice, however, it more often turns into a burning issue that needs to be resolved. Two factors can be to blame.

The first is that the organization's characteristic style of communication may be at odds with more modern norms of acceptability. For instance, where once it was accepted for managers to hand down orders from on high, nowadays we believe in agreeing on performance targets. And where once we felt elected officials were within their rights to withhold comment, now we expect journalists to cross-examine and even contradict them, at least in modern democracies.

A second factor is that the organization's words and actions may not be aligned. What a person says or writes, and therefore promises, has to coincide with the behavior they display. If these two things clash, it destroys credibility and trust. As every public relations expert will tell you, you have to practice what you preach.

Take car manufacturers and their talk of sustainability, all vying with each other to claim the cleanest image. But that talk turned out to be just a lot of hot air when in 2015 it was discovered that Volkswagen had manipulated the software in its diesel cars to appear to comply with U.S. environmental standards. That was a big mistake, blowing up into a scandal of epic proportions, and one not limited to Volkswagen alone. The impact was huge and eroded trust in whole the automotive industry. We see this every day: organizations, politicians, and others failing to practice what they preach even though we know how fundamental it is to winning and retaining trust.

The importance of corporate character—on which the Arthur W. Page Society (among others) has done significant research in recent years—is impossible to overstate. After all, it encompasses the definition and alignment of the mission, purpose, values, culture, business model, strategy, operations, and brand to create the unique, differentiating identity of the enterprise.

COMMUNICATION STYLE IMPACTS THE ROLE OF THE COMMMUNICATION DEPARTMENT

Much as with corporate silence, signaling issues in the organization's communication style tends to be seen as a job for communication professionals, including getting it on the management agenda and confronting others in the organization with their behavior. But these are treacherous waters. Before you know it, people might start questioning your mandate and telling you to mind your own business.

If style is a burning issue in your organization, you may want to consider forming a united front with other departments to draw attention to the issue. By forging a coalition with HR or the strategy team, for example, you can avoid making a stand alone or becoming isolated.

Organizations' style of communicating and interacting is getting an increasing amount of attention these days, but unfortunately most discussions fail to delve below the surface, treating it as a matter of technique and training. Moreover, organizations usually have not one, but many different styles of interacting. If you want to address this, the best approach is to start cautiously, with one department that is obviously struggling, showing signs of infighting or poor performance. Defining effective, management-backed communication standards in your vision from the very outset can be a big help.

Inhouse communication styles often also affect how people think about the communication department's role within the organization. If that style is directive, then the communication professional will likewise be expected to take a directive (read: one-sided persuasive) approach. If instead it is very conversational, then people will automatically expect informality from their communication team. If the organizational style centers on co-creation, then collaboration, reaching out, and forming coalitions will be what is expected of you. If the style is invitational, then the organization will naturally be more receptive to the public mood and whatever issues may come along, which then also opens the way for the more reflective role of monitoring and second-order management as described by the communication scholar Howard Nothhaft (2010). In short, an organization's inhouse communication style is fundamentally tied to the latitude it gives its communication professionals and the style in which they can approach their work.

10 DO'S AND DON'TS

1   Don't restrict yourself to listing your organization's mission, ambitions, and objectives. Make an effort to truly understand what they mean from a communication perspective. Also continue to reiterate them in discussions, plans, and recommendations to make them come alive.

2   Do make sure to stay keyed in to what is happening in the boardroom. Ideally, you should be talking with the management board members themselves. If not, connect with people who do have board access.

3   Don't limit your horizons to the head office: stay up on important developments at subsidiaries and in the workplaces. In other words, cultivate a network of informants.

4   Do your homework by reading key strategic documents carefully and stay informed.

5   Do gather information not only at your computer but by engaging and talking with all levels of the organization. Show your face.

6   Don't look only at what is explicit (tip of the iceberg), but also be alert to things happening "under the surface." Talk around the water cooler or coffee machine can also be an important source of information.

7   Do share key insights with both your coworkers and other people in the organization.

8   Do maintain a list of the main issues and keep it up to date. You can also prioritize issues by "probability" (likelihood it will get worse) and "impact on the organization."

9   Do be well prepared: keep an eye on internal developments and identify how they might impact communication. That way, you'll never be surprised.

10 Do explicitly define the acceptable inhouse communication style, and if you haven't already done so in your vision, distinguish between the actual and the desired communication style.

THE INTERNAL SITUATION BUILDING BLOCK HELPS YOU TO ASK CRITICAL QUESTIONS ABOUT THE INTERNAL SITUATION AND ORGANIZATIONAL INTERACTION. KNOWING THIS IS ESSENTIAL FOR AN EFFECTIVE COMMUNICATION STRATEGY.

STRATEGIZING AND PLANNING ARE CONTINUOUS CONCERNS

DEJAN VERČIČ **ON COMMUNICATION STRATEGY**

COMMUNICATION STRATEGY

THERE IS ALWAYS A MULTITUDE OF FUTURES IN FRONT OF US, AND STRATE-GIES ARE WAYS OF THEIR ENACTMENTS. AS MUCH AS OUR UNDERSTANDING OF POTENTIAL OPTIONS AND STAKEHOLDER COORDINATION ARE COMMU-NICATIVELY COPRODUCED, STRATEGIC COMMUNICATION PLANNING BRINGS SOME DISCIPLINE TO OTHERWISE STOCHASTIC FLOW OF TIME.

STRATEGY IS ALWAYS WORK IN PROGRESS, AND WHAT IS OF THE UTMOST IMPORTANCE IS PLANNING AS THE PROCESS, NOT PLANS AS PRODUCTS. ALL WINS (AND LOSES) ARE TEMPORAL, AND FOR THAT REASON STARTEGISING AND PLANING ARE CONNTINUOUS CONCERNS.

BEING ABLE TO EMPLOY MODELS FOR RECOGNISING STRUCTURATION OF VARIOUS FUTURES IN FRONT OF YOU AND BEING ABLE TO CHECK FAST VARIOUS AVAILABLE ROUTES YOU COULD TAKE INCREASES REQUISITE VA-RIETY OF CHOICES YOU CAN MAKE, AND THUS IMPROVES YOUR CHANCE OF SURVIVAL AND GROWTH.

Dejan Verčič, Ph.D.
Professor and Head of the Department of Communication,
University of Ljubljana, Slovenia
Partner and Knowledge Director at Stratkom d.o.o., Slovenia

BUILDING BLOCK
EXTERNAL SITUATION

Communication professionals are sometimes described as having one foot in and one foot outside the organization. It follows that communication departments should be able to look ahead and recognize relevant trends, developments, and issues, to gauge public sentiment about issues that are important to the organization, and be knowledgeable about the typical behaviors of key groups. This not only reinforces its day-to-day credibility, but also gives the department a better handle on its priorities.

A cursory glance at the newspapers should be enough to convince any organization of the importance of being attuned to the external environment. We've all read the headlines. An executive's severance package reduced in deference to "sensitivities surrounding severance pay." A big bank under fire for plans to share client data with companies despite ongoing privacy concerns. An American food manufacturer that pulls out of Europe following widespread criticism and protests against genetically manipulated seeds. Every organization has its own issues and occasionally finds itself in the crosshairs of public debate. Sometimes it blows over, but every so often it continues to simmer, or the sparks begin to fly and the organization is rocked to its foundations.

Most organizations operate in quite a turbulent playing field. To excel as a communication expert, you have to understand that playing field. If you don't know what is happening around you or get caught off guard by the public mood on pivotal issues, you may suddenly find yourself facing a massive problem. On the other hand, if you are attuned to what is happening and you are able to harness that knowledge to your benefit, then you can help the organization or your client to get ahead.

MOST ORGANIZATIONS OPERATE IN QUITE A TURBULENT PLAYING FIELD. TO EXCEL
AS A COMMUNICATION EXPERT, YOU HAVE TO UNDERSTAND THAT PLAYING FIELD.

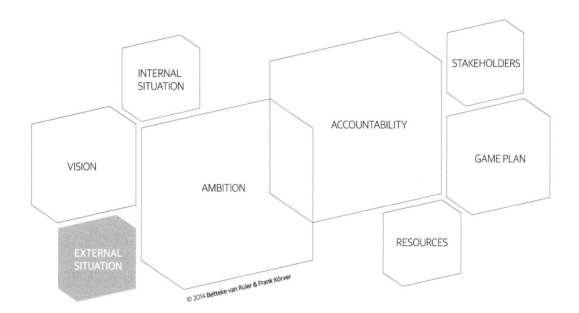

© 2014 Betteke van Ruler & Frank Körver

**THE EXTERNAL ENVIRONMENT PLAYS A CENTRAL ROLE IN YOUR STRA-
TEGY, SO DEVELOP YOUR STRATEGY WITH THAT IN MIND BY CONSIDE-
RING AT LEAST THESE TWO QUESTIONS:**

1   What are relevant societal trends and developments?
2   What are relevant issues, and what is the public mood about them?

◥ Beware!
*The major risk of analyses like this is that you merely seek to confirm what you
already knew. Discovering the unexpected is by far the biggest feat, says Nassim Nicholas Taleb in* The Black Swan *(2008). To achieve that, you need a broad
foundation of general knowledge, an inquisitive mindset, and a creative spirit.*

5 KICKSTARTERS

1 WHAT RELEVANT TOPICS HAVE CONSISTENTLY DOMINATED THE NEWS OR BEEN TRENDING TOPICS IN ONLINE NEWS GROUPS? AND WHAT IS THE TENOR OF THOSE DISCUSSIONS?

2 WHAT TRENDS AND DEVELOPMENTS ARE CITED IN KEY SECTOR REPORTS? WHAT DOES THE INDUSTRY ASSOCIATION OR PROFESSIONAL FEDERATION IDENTIFY AS TRENDS TO WATCH?

3 TRACK OF FEAR: WHAT TRENDS, DEVELOPMENTS OR ISSUES WORRY YOU OR YOUR COWORKERS?

4 TRACK OF HOPE: WHAT TRENDS, DEVELOPMENTS, OR ISSUES PROMISE INTERESTING OPPORTUNITIES?

5 AT WHAT TRENDS, DEVELOPMENTS, OR ISSUES ARE COMPETITORS AIMING THEIR EFFORTS?

SOCIETAL TRENDS AND DEVELOPMENTS

A communication professional should have a good nose for significant trends and developments, particularly where it concerns trends and developments that will or could impact the organization and that have a bearing on communication. This is not to say you have to be a trendwatcher or avid reader of sector reports, but a professional certainly cannot develop strategies with blinders on. Factoring in relevant trends and developments enables you to maximize opportunities, and also to avoid running unnecessary risks.

Rather than tracking every trend or trying to single out the main ones, the trick is to distinguish what is important for your own organization. Information is power, and that adage applies equally to trends. If you are informed about the issues, then you can plan ahead. The challenge lies in making an intelligent selection of the main trends and developments, and then looking at them through the lens of communication and asking: How will this impact our communication?

- **What trends and developments could strike at the heart of our organization?**
  Primarily, these are trends and developments that impact on the positioning, proposition, or strategy of the enterprise or its identity. For instance, the Big Five corporations—Facebook, Google, Microsoft, Amazon, and Apple—will keep close tabs on any discussions about privacy and competition.

- **What trends and developments are relevant from the content perspective?**
  Some trends and developments are significant mainly as they pertain to content strategy. For many food manufacturers, but also supermarkets, for instance, discussions about food safety make it crucial to highlight where ingredients are sourced. By keying in to trends and developments, you can establish or bolster your position.

- **What trends and developments are relevant from the customer or stakeholder perspective?**
  Some trends and developments mainly affect stakeholders, but are still relevant to communication. Take the increasing tendency among politicians to play to their electorate by adopting a more hardline and populist stance on issues, which can have massive consequences for an organization wrestling with diversity policies.

- **What trends and developments are relevant from the perspective of the professional field of practice?**
  Many trends and developments influence the field of communication. Social media have by now evolved from trend to daily practice, but current debates over the rise of branded journalism, fake news, and applications of big data can still generate new ideas and insights.

Determining which trends and developments are relevant may not even be the biggest challenge—the toughest thing is to make intelligent use of all the data at your fingertips. These days there is no shortage of books and websites detailing the trends that will reshape society, while data about everything under the sun is readily available within organizations and openly accessible outside them. Therefore, our advice is to spare yourself the effort of becoming a trendwatcher and instead use the knowledge that has already been collected. But, as always, be selective.

Lots of organizations have already identified their trends to watch, so before you reinvent the wheel, ask around in the organization whether key trends and developments have already been mapped out. That way, you can align with existing efforts. But also do your homework. Keep an ear open and an eye out for what opinion leaders in your industry are saying and writing. Read sector reports and

---

WHAT CAN YOU DO ABOUT BURNING ISSUES?
These days, organizations have to be more attuned than ever to the quality of their relationship with society at large, especially as that relationship seems to be subject to increasing pressures. What role should communication play? What if a burning issue arises between the organization and its stakeholders? There are three ways in which a communication team or department can make meaningful contributions:

- As an expert advisor it can help to improve decision-making and/or change behaviors by sharing specific insights with senior management ("Our organization has to address this differently" or "We need to let things settle first").

- In the event of a misunderstanding, it can try to change how the organization is perceived ("The public has misjudged us").

- It can try to rectify the public's expectations ("The public has the wrong idea").

relevant research. Follow the media, and especially read the trade journals that zoom in on issues in your sector. Regularly set aside an afternoon to spend on this research, which will keep you sharp and provide inspiration. And remember that your purpose in all of this is to figure out: How does this impact communication?

Your aim is to identify trends and developments that you believe are or could be relevant to your work. We cannot stress this enough. That means you have to make choices. It goes without saying that the choices you make will influence your Game Plan (see that building block). As we've said before, all elements of the Communication Strategy Framework are made to work together.

ISSUES AND STAKEHOLDERS
Every organization sometimes finds itself facing an expectation gap around certain issues or topics. Your organization says or does X while your stakeholders expected you to say or do Y. If you fail to close this gap in time, the situation could unleash a wave of public indignation. You have to not only keep track of those issues, but also identify and monitor any tensions they induce in stakeholders.

But how do you know if something is a real issue? To figure this out, you have to gauge three things: the likelihood that a topic will escalate to become a full-blown issue, the issue's relevance to the organization, its operations, or products and services, and the impact that public discussion about the issue could have on the organization. There is no rulebook for this; your team simply has to evaluate each situation as it comes. There is one tip we can give you, however: the earlier you signal an issue, the better. If the media are talking about it, you are probably too late. In the worst case, your organization will be scrambling to catch up while your competitor's swift response turns the issue to their advantage.

Issues have a life cycle. Most start in the private domain, in a disagreement over some topic about which a small group of people becomes increasingly vocal. After a critical mass has been reached, institutional actors get involved. NGOs enter the fray and task forces are created. The issue escalates, increasing the chances it will cross over into the public domain. It sparks a broad social dialogue, especially once the media get in on the action. By this point it has become a full-blown issue. There are calls for policy measures. When laws and regulations are formulated to deal with the issue, it becomes part of the government domain, and because those laws and regulations have been instated, now there is a normative judgment about the issue—an official decision on what is right and wrong. At this stage the issue usually fades from view. It could surge back to life if there are violations, and then it may return, or it may prove to have run its course.

Social media have significantly cut the life cycle of issues because they can catapult them from the private domain straight into the traditional media or even the political arena.

Issues can escalate very rapidly, and that makes issue management tricky. Now more than ever, you have to flag and prioritize issues as early as possible. To do that, however, you already need to have established what is and is not important. Naturally, this is different for every organization. To be able to assess what is important, you need to have broad knowledge, an inquisitive mindset, and a clear picture of what is happening both in the wider world and within your organization.

WHY DO WE FAIL TO SEE ISSUES ARISE?
In *MIT Sloan Management Review,* Paul J. H. Schoemaker and George S. Day (2009) explain why many organizations fail to see changes and threats coming in time or at all. Their research revealed that less than 20% of global firms have sufficient capacity to spot, interpret, and act on the weak signals of forthcoming threats and opportunities. Based on their article, we can identify three factors that blind us to important issues:

- **Filtering:** Where we focus our attention is determined mainly by what we expect to see. That is, we filter information as it comes to us. This is called selective perception. When something does not tally or align with our way of thinking, our brains reshape reality to make it fit.

- **Bolstering:** As well as filtering all the information we receive, we also cherry-pick the information that supports our ideas and point of view. Thus, we end up interacting mostly with people who agree with us and are inclined to seek out evidence that reinforces our perspective.

- **Groupthink:** You would think that groups should be better equipped than lone individuals to point out changes. They're not. Members of a group are more likely to value the "we" feeling and therefore are less likely to voice criticisms or admit information that contradicts the group viewpoint.

From:
MIT Sloan Management Review, 2009

"Filter bubbles" are something that has gotten a lot of attention lately. This is where algorithms are used to feed us more of the information we already consume and that squares with our existing opinions and beliefs. The impact of filter bubbles can be huge, certainly when it drives wedges between groups of people.

So, what does this mean? As a communication professional, you are the person who has to hold a mirror up to the organization. Your knowledge about stakeholder concerns and what the media are talking about puts you in a position to ask critical questions, influence decision-making, and keep the organization's management from growing blind to crucial developments.

PUBLIC MOOD

Public sentiment or mood describes what certain groups think about certain matters. These sentiments can be about the industry as a whole, the organization, or the product, or about a CEO or management behavior. Public mood is never static; it shifts over time and can differ in different contexts, depending on what the issue is, which can make it tough to get and keep a clear grasp of what the mood is surrounding key issues. The best way to keep a finger on the public pulse is to listen closely to how stakeholders talk about those issues with one another. That is, through content and discourse analysis.

Public opinion, as Jürgen Habermas (1962) wrote in his German classic *Strukturwandel der Oeffentlichkeit,* is the opinion that is constructed and expressed openly, in the public sphere. He contrasted this with the private sphere; the home. In principle, everybody has access to the public sphere and this is the arena where public opinions are formed, according to Habermas, by means of a critical, rational debate. Though widely attacked, his theory that public opinion is always premised on a critical and rational debate has nevertheless shaped subsequent discussions. Partly for that reason, we prefer to use the term public mood or sentiment. Opinion is about value judgments—legitimate or not, as the case may be. Mood and sentiment are about emotion. Rational debate is something most organizations can manage; mood is a good deal thornier.

SOCIONOMICS

Socionomics is a field of science concerned with the analysis of social moods, based on the understanding that these largely drive events in society. If that is true, then socionomics could be very valuable for communication professionals.

ORGANIZATIONAL LISTENING

Despite the use of Web 2.0-based social media and an ideology of dialogue and conversation, there is still a huge lack of listening and dialogue in organizational communication, as Australian communication scholar Jim Macnamara (2016) shows in his book *Organizational Listening: The Missing Essential in Public Communication.* These days, the Internet and social media have made it relatively easy to follow and analyze public conversations. But let's keep our focus broad. Because not everything is evident, not all issues can be pared down to 280 characters, and not all public moods are captured by social media. For instance, a geriatric care organization is better off focusing its analyses on face-to-face discussions, because many seniors probably won't use the Internet to express their opinions. The same is true of employees; they, too, will be less likely to broadcast certain views. Keeping your ears open in the office canteen or during post-meeting chitchat can yield a treasure trove of information about the internal social mood. These are the social stories inside the organization. Similarly, conversations at parties and the local café or on newspaper and quote sites reveal the social stories happening in the outside world, and offer a barometer of the external public mood. Incidentally, behavioral observation and content or conversation analysis often tell you a lot more than surveys do, but they are still rarely used by communication specialists. If you ask us, that's a wasted opportunity!

WHAT REALLY MATTERS TO STAKEHOLDERS

In 2013, John Browne and Robin Nuttall published an article in McKinsey Quarterly about how organizations are putting far too much effort into trying to convince others that their actions are legitimate, instead of into listening to and trying to understand the things that concern and matter to their stakeholders. The authors quote Helge Lund, CEO of Statoil, who said, "Knowing your stakeholders means more than writing down a list of risks they could pose, having a cup of tea with some NGO heads, and holding a few focus groups. It means understanding your stakeholders as rigorously as you understand your consumers." The authors demonstrate that rigorously understanding your stakeholders helps to cement strong ties. Effective external engagement relies on a detailed knowledge of the preferences and resources of stakeholders, they claim. "That means learning, on an individual and institutional level, what they want, why they want it, how much they are prepared to compromise, how your activities affect their goals, and what resources and influence they can bring to bear." As we all know: it takes two to tango.

┐ Read it here:

"Beyond corporate social responsibility: Integrated external engagement"
http://alturl.com/ab5ah

10 DO'S AND DON'TS

1   Do limit yourself to the three to five main trends and developments and three to five main issues. In other words, make choices. Use a risk matrix with a probability axis and an impact axis to help you.

2   Don't treat the identification of trends, developments, and issues as a one-off exercise; always keep one finger on the public pulse.

3   Do get key people in the organization (at all levels) involved in defining the most important trends, developments, and issues.

4   Don't rely on only a single source. Instead, do a meta-analysis of the most reliable and authoritative sources to distill a compact set of relevant trends, developments, and issues.

5   Don't reinvent the wheel: use the information that is already out there.

6   Do draw attention to significant shifts, and make it clear how they might affect the organization. And, if the situation merits it, sound the alarm—but not too often.

7   Don't underestimate the impact that developments can have, but also don't overprioritize every trend, development, or issue that crosses your radar.

8   Do focus on the facts: use authoritative sources and cite them in the documents you produce.

9   Forge coalitions to get key issues on the senior management's agenda. This is especially important if you expect any resistance.

10 Do know what pitfalls you might encounter when pointing out trends and be conscious of the role that you as a communication professional can play to break through patterns (filtering, groupthink, bolstering).

TO UNDERSTAND THE EXTERNAL SITUATION, YOU NEED INSIGHT INTO THE RELE-
VANT TRENDS AND DEVELOPMENTS, THE ISSUES, AND THE PUBLIC MOOD. RATHER
THAN COLLECTING LOTS OF DATA, THE TRICK IS TO DISTINGUISH WHAT IS CRUCIAL
FOR YOUR OWN ORGANIZATION AND ITS COMMUNICATIONS.

CONTROL IS SOMETHING OF THE PAST, ENABLING HAS GOT TO BE THE NEW GAME

COMMUNICATION
STRATEGY

TODAY'S REALITY IS A CHALLENGING ONE: SDGs, CLIMATE CHANGE, BIODI-
VERSITY LOSS AND A REFUGEE CRISIS ALL OVER THE WORLD. ON TOP OF
THAT WE HAVE FAKE NEWS, INCREASING NEW DIGITAL REALITIES WITH AI
AND VR AND A 24-HOURS SOCIAL MEDIA DYNAMIC.

CONTROL IS SOMETHING OF THE PAST, ENABLING HAS GOT TO BE THE NEW
GAME AND LISTENING IS MORE IMPORTANT THAN EVER. SECTORAL BOUN-
DARIES ARE BLURRING. NGOS HAVE BECOME MARKETING MACHINES AND
COMPANIES ARE PRACTICING THEIR ADVOCACY VOICE. WAS THERE EVER
A GREATER NEED FOR INTEGRATING THE COMMUNICATION AND BUSINESS
STRATEGIES AND BE TRULY AUTHENTIC?

I HAVE BEEN ADVOCATING FOR THE 3As COMMUNICATIONS CONCEPT:
AUTHENTICITY, ACCOUNTABILITY AND AUDACITY. FIRST A: STAND FOR WHAT
YOU DO AND WHO YOU TRULY ARE. SECOND A: INTEGRATE BEING ACCOUN-
TABLE TO MOTHER EARTH AND FUTURE GENERATIONS. THIRD A: TO DO THE
FIRST TWO, ONE NEEDS TO BE AUDACIOUS.

THIS CONCEPT WILL ENSURE A BUSINESS DISCUSSION AND SUPPORT MA-
KING THE RIGHT CHOICES FOR A PURPOSEFUL FUTURE.

Inge Wallage
Managing Director
European Association of Communication Directors (EACD),
Owner of The Butterfly Effect, Strategies for Transformation, Amsterdam,
The Netherlands

BUILDING BLOCK
AMBITION

To be ambitious means you are always trying to improve. You keep on raising the bar higher and are willing to fight to attain your goal. Good ambitions are inspiring and articulate what you want to achieve and at the same time indicate how you will achieve it. Whatever your game plan, there is always an implicit ambition. By making it explicit, you can assess whether your game plan is founded on the right ambition, and vice versa. Whereas objectives describe specifically what you want to accomplish within a given time frame, ambitions describe your core task; how high you are setting the bar and what you want to attain over the long term. In effect, ambitions provide guideposts for your specific near-term objectives and actions. But we will get to that in the Game Plan building block.

Ambition also says something about your method; about pursuing a particular objective in a conscious, deliberate, and concentrated way. Equally, it refers to the objective itself—to what you are striving for—and hence crystallizes what your department, team, or you as a professional want to achieve. Being ambitious is not just about craving success, but about being committed to something. At this stage, that something might not be fully defined yet, nor does it need to be, but there does have to be a clear and inspiring destination you ultimately hope to reach, your objectives or goals.

Underpinning every ambition is a set of beliefs and ideas that validate the objective. Without that underpinning, you will not be able to take purposeful or deliberate action. This is something we already discussed in detail in the building block about Vision. Here, however, we want to zoom in on the core values and core task that go with your situation outline and on the situation or moment in time for which you are creating your strategy. Within the Communication Strategy Framework, the Ambition building block therefore follows logically from the buildings blocks about Vision, Internal Situation, and External Situation.

CORE VALUES TRANSLATE YOUR VISION TO YOUR CURRENT CIRCUMSTANCES, ARTICULATING WHAT YOU STAND FOR. THE CORE TASKS ARTICULATE WHAT YOU WANT TO ATTAIN.

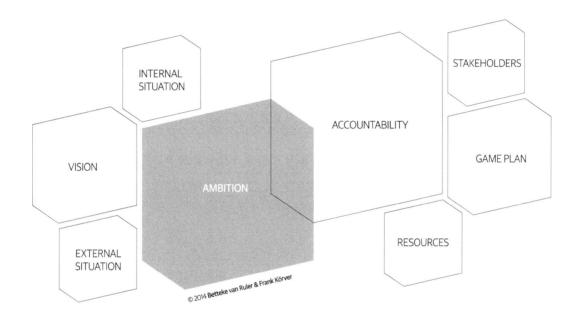

© 2014 Betteke van Ruler & Frank Körver

TO FORMULATE A WORKING AMBITION, YOU HAVE TO ANSWER TWO QUESTIONS:

1 What are our core tasks or what do we want to accomplish in the time ahead or in this situation?
2 What are the core values driving our efforts?

⌐ Beware!
Formulating a clear ambition requires more than merely adding up the results of the previous three building blocks. It also demands conceptual creativity, thinking outside the box, and a strategic mentality. In other words, you have to apply a combination of both creativity and logic.

5 KICKSTARTERS

1   WHICH ORGANIZATIONS COMMUNICATE IN A WAY THAT APPEALS TO YOU, AND WHAT MAKES THEIR COMMUNICATION APPEALING?

2   HOW COULD YOU, AS COMMUNICATION PROFESSIONALS, MAKE A REAL DIFFERENCE IN THE ORGANIZATION OR IN A PROJECT? WHAT WOULD MAKE YOU TRULY INDISPENSIBLE?

3   FOR WHAT ACHIEVEMENT WITHIN YOUR CURRENT CONTEXT WOULD YOU LIKE TO BE RECOGNIZED BY FELLOW PROFESSIONALS? AND BY YOUR ORGANIZATION?

4   HOW DO YOU DEFINE EXCELLENT? HOW DO YOU DEFINE EXCELLENT COMMUNICATION AMBITIONS?

5   IF YOU HAD TO SPEND YOUR WHOLE BUDGET TO ATTAIN JUST ONE OBJECTIVE, WHAT WOULD IT BE?

CORE VALUES

Core values can be a great tool because they articulate precisely what you stand for. As your own or your team's professional signature, they effectively define your position. But to do that, they have to be explicit and they have to be specific enough to make it clear what kind of actions are expected from the department and anyone else involved in communication.

These days, practically every organization has a set of explicit core values. Often, thanks to the communication department, which directs or facilitates the process of formulating core values, or—though we don't recommend it—actually formulates and supplies these themselves. This is a typical job for the communication profession. Oddly enough, however, those core values do not always play an equally explicit role in the communication department itself. Rarely, furthermore, are core values formulated specifically to govern communication, let alone for specific circumstances in which a strategy may be needed. Why not? After all, formulating core values is a highly effective way of signaling how you want to add value; they tell your story, or the story about your policy, and lay a basis for your communication Game Plan.

WHAT ARE THE CORE VALUES OF MY COMMUNICATION DEPARTMENT?
What might those core values be? We have come across our fair share and the following are some we particularly like. For clarity's sake, we have formulated them all the same way:

- We are accountable; we can demonstrate how we contribute to achieving the organization's objectives.

- We are a positive stimulus; we think in terms of opportunities that we can capitalize on and always stay one step ahead of the organization.

- We are proud of our professionalism and the service we provide; we serve the organization without making concessions in our professionalism.

- We are entrepreneurial advisors; we reach out to the outside world and actively seek out ways in which we can make the difference.

- We know what is happening and are proactive; because we know what is happening in and outside the organization, we can proactively advise our internal customers about the most effective communication Game Plan.

- We are responding to the current situation by being extra inviting and focused on dialogue in the period ahead.

TRANSLATION OF YOUR VISION

Solid core values give you a collective frame of reference. In the section on Vision
we wrote about the importance of weighing every word, because the language
in which you define your vision matters. The same applies when formulating core
values, which are the translation of your vision to a particular situation or moment
in time. Your core values have to answer the question: What are we doing, and why
are we doing it? It is not enough to merely write down your core values; you have
to explain them too, preferably in the form of a few catchphrases that are easy to
remember, energize you, and maybe even coax a smile. Even better, visualize your
core values, giving them a symbolic face so they will be more memorable. Core
values also have to be borne out in your advising style and behaviors, in all your
actions and your leadership. The proof of your core values is in the implementation, which reveals to what extent they have been internalized. If your day-to-day
actions don't square with your core values, those values will only seem ridiculous.

CORE TASK

The core task is the specific thing that needs to be achieved on the communication
front. In effect, it is your department's current reason for existing. You might call
it a target, but we prefer to steer clear of that term here because it tends to make
people think in figures or percentages. Your core task follows from your analysis of
the external and internal situations, is inspired by your vision and core values, and
delineates precisely what the communication department wants to achieve on the
communication front in a given situation or time period.

How do you go about formulating a core task? Whereas the task itself is wholly
dependent on the results of the first three building blocks, we can offer some
guidelines as to the formulation. First and foremost, it has to be as specific as
possible. Your aim is to state clearly and plainly what your task is; thus, what you
intend to accomplish. Just as when formulating your core values, keep it short and
simple. Be concrete. Also important is to distinguish between output and impact.
Sometimes departments formulate core tasks like "We produce creative means of
communication," or "We create stakeholder dialogue," or "We advise management
about the brand and reputation." These only describe output. We're not a fan of
these kinds of core tasks because they say nothing about what the impact is supposed to be, which of course is the whole point.

We are a fan of moonshots. People who think in terms of moonshots are not interested in boosting performance by 10%, or 30%, but by a factor of ten at the very

CORE VALUE QUIZ

Imagine that your communication department has summed up its core values as "customer-focused, innovative, and responsible for results." How do you establish whether all department members are upholding these values? This quiz is inspired by one used in change management and adapted to measure to what extent communication is living up to its core values. The seven questions are scored on a scale of 1 to 6, where 1 stands for not or hardly present and 6 for completely present. Naturally, the specific questions you ask will depend on the core values you choose, but you can use these as a guide.

QUIZ: CUSTOMER-FOCUSED, INNOVATIVE, AND RESPONSIBLE FOR RESULTS

Do communication staff know what internal customers think of their services?	1 2 3 4 5 6
Are the wishes of internal customers discussed at team meetings?	1 2 3 4 5 6
Are new developments in the services provided discussed within the team?	1 2 3 4 5 6
Does the team have insight into its own costs, outputs, and outcomes?	1 2 3 4 5 6
Are team members interested in the above factors?	1 2 3 4 5 6
Do these values contribute to constructive discussions within the team?	1 2 3 4 5 6
Do these values lead to specific agreements and actions for improvement?	1 2 3 4 5 6

least. In other words, they shoot for the moon—or, like Elon Musk more recently, Mars. Of course, you have to be careful not to overreach, but many problems are actually easier to solve if you strive for radical improvement rather than just an easy fix.

FOCUS, FOCUS, FOCUS

How many core tasks can a department have? In theory, as many as it wants, but it is more practical to concentrate on just a few. First, because otherwise they risk becoming too profuse. Second, because you, your department, or your agency have to be realistically able to invest the necessary time and effort in these tasks, and moreover to deliver. You might also consider formulating one core task for your ongoing work and others for the given situation or period.

Communication departments often have two core tasks: one directed inward, toward the organization, and another directed outward, toward the outside world. Sometimes, they have more than two. Our advice remains to strive for focus. Make choices. Limit yourself to three or at most four core tasks. Also, avoid jargon. Your core task has to be easy to understand, easy to remember, and easy to reproduce, both for the people in your department and those outside it.

STRONG CORE TASKS

"We help our organization to achieve its goals by making it a powerful brand and by strengthening ties between the organization's staff and its external target groups."

"We put our organization on the map and make employees proud of the organization."

"We create a communicative organization that knows how to capitalize on reputation opportunity and avoid reputation risk."

These are examples of strong core tasks, because the results are about real impact. What do you want to achieve? Your output—what your department makes, produces, or supplies—is the means to achieve that impact, and is discussed in the Game Plan building block.

START THINKING ABOUT YOUR PUBLIC

Whatever you call the people you wish to communicate with—your target group, publics, partners, or co-creators—it is vital when fleshing out your strategy to start thinking about where you want to aim it. Who is or will be important, who do you need to keep an eye on, who do you always need to listen to, who do you need to bring on board or keep in the loop, who is displaying behaviors you may want to address or attitudes that could present a problem? Your analysis of the issues and stakeholders should have crystallized who these groups are, but it is wise to give them some additional thought at this stage as that will make it easier to flesh out your ambition in your stakeholder analysis and game plan. If you still don't have an adequate grasp of the people you ultimately want to communicate with, then you will have to do more research. After all, you will not be able to develop a solid communication strategy if you don't fully understand what motivates your target groups.

DEFINITION OF DONE

The scrum method teaches us that when starting the planning process it is crucial to think ahead and ask: What do I need to accomplish to be satisfied? This "definition of done" is like a checklist that specifies the criteria your end product has to meet for you to be satisfied. It can also help if you are having trouble formulating focused ambitions: start with your definition of done and then reason your way backwards.

10 DO'S AND DON'TS

1   Don't think in terms of limitations, but in opportunities.

2   Do try to step outside your comfort zone; ambitions have to be both challenging and appealing.

3   Do dare to dream. By dreaming together, you can make your core task and ambitions come alive.

4   Do let others test your ambitions. Are you being too modest? Or are your expectations unrealistic?

5   Do keep reiterating your ambitions to keep them fresh in your mind. Take a tip from advertising: repetition works.

6   Don't underestimate the importance of an appealing core task and clear ambitions. They not only point the way, but also provide a touchstone.

7   Do formulate core values and core tasks using language that inspires, and avoid jargon. Symbolism can be a useful tool, and visualization can help.

8   Do take your ambitions very seriously; only apply them when there are valid reasons to do so, and then do it with conviction.

9   Do assess how your core values and core tasks will impact the team and the rest of the organization; how do they play into the desired employee mindset?

10 Do try to make your ambitions specific by connecting them to stakeholders. In other words: what do you want to change in the hearts and minds of your stakeholder groups?

THE AMBITION BUILDING BLOCK IS ABOUT WHAT YOU WANT TO ACHIEVE AND WHAT YOU STAND FOR: CORE TASKS AND CORE VALUES. WHAT YOU WANT TO ACHIEVE IS OUTLINED IN THE CHOICES YOU MAKE IN THE FIRST THREE BUILDING BLOCKS. ARE YOU UNABLE TO FORMULATE FOCUSED AMBITIONS? THEN NINE TIMES OUT OF TEN, THE CHOICES YOU MADE IN THE FIRST THREE BUILDING BLOCKS WERE NOT TARGETED ENOUGH.

BIG DATA HAS IMPELLED A STRATEGIC SHIFT

XIANHONG CHEN **ON COMMUNICATION STRATEGY**

COMMUNICATION STRATEGY

IN-DEPTH INTERVIEWS BASED ON GROUNDED THEORY OF 30 CHINESE PUBLIC RELATIONS SCHOLARS IN THE GREATER CHINA REGION SHOWED THAT THE BIG DATA ERA HAS IMPELLED A STRATEGIC SHIFT IN EDUCATION, RESEARCH AND PRACTICE IN PUBLIC RELATIONS.

THERE EXISTS AN INTERESTING "BESIEGED CITY" PHENOMENON MANIFES-TING THE TENSION BETWEEN "DE-INSTITUTIONALIZING PUBLIC RELATIONS" AND "INSTITUTIONALIZING PUBLIC RELATIONS". THE DEBATE OF "DOWN-PLAYING NEWS" AND "UP-PLAYING PR" APPEARED IN COMMUNICATION EDU-CATION. BIG DATA PROPELLED THE EMERGENCE OF A TENDENCY TO BEING INTEGRATED, TRANSDISCIPLINARY AND STRATEGIC. STRATEGIC SHIFTS DO NOT NECESSARILY SYNCHRONIZE. THEY CAN ALSO BE SEEN AS THE EXPRES-SION OF ATTEMPTS OR EFFORTS TO MAKE ALL PUBLIC RELATIONS BECOME STRATEGIC IN THE CONTEXT OF EQUATING PUBLIC RELATIONS TO STRATEGY.

THE CONCEPT OF "PUBLIC RELATIONS IS STRATEGY" MEANS THAT ALL PU-BLIC RELATIONS ACTIONS SHOULD BE WELL PLANNED AND GUIDED. FROM THIS PERSPECTIVE, STRATEGY IS NOT SIMPLY A VARIABLE AMONG OTHERS.

STRATEGY IS WHAT PUBLIC RELATIONS IS INTENDED TO.

Xianhong Chen, Ph.D.
President of China Public Relations Association
Professor at the School of Journalism and Communication
of Huazhong University of Science and Technology, Wuhan, China

IMPLEMENTATION: THE RIGHT PART OF THE COMMUNICATION STRATEGY FRAMEWORK

A closer look at the right part of the model: Accountability, Stakeholders, Resources, and Game Plan.

ACCOUNTABILITY

Being accountable means you leave no doubt about who is responsible for what, and how, and how and to whom you answer. Simply stated, it is about showing who is in charge of what and in what way, and what the things you do will deliver.

STAKEHOLDERS

In the communication field we talk a lot about the stakeholders in the organization. Rarely, however, do we talk about the stakeholders in the communication strategy itself. Who do you need to ensure your strategy's success, and what do you need from them?

RESOURCES

The Resources building block centers on people and money. You may have big ambitions, but you also have to be realistic. Increasingly, departments are expected to do more with less money and less personnel. You can only do that if you make decisive choices and know exactly which competences and budgetary scope you need to achieve your ambitions.

GAME PLAN

The Game Plan building block is about putting the finishing touches on your strategy. What is your approach? This is what we call your operational strategy, or tactics, and requires you to define your working methods, and set priorities.

Figure 5. Right part of the Communication Strategy Framework

BUILDING BLOCK
ACCOUNTABILITY

Having an ambition without constantly showing that you are doing the right things in the right way is no more than just a dream (Bettag, 2014, p. 15). In public relations and communication management, evaluation serves to demonstrate that your department is an investment, and not merely an expense, but even more to demonstrate that you contribute to the organizational objectives, and thus that you want to be accountable to others. "Being accountable is essential in order to be a 'need-to-have' communication department rather than a 'nice-to-have' department, but little attention is paid to what accountability really is," argue Carlijn Remmelzwaal, Caroline Wehrmann, and Frank Körver (2015).

John Roberts and Robert Scapens (1985) were the first to view accountability as a requirement to both explain and take responsibility for actions. This definition of accountability echoes Drucker's "are we doing the right things and are we doing these in the right way?" Under this broad definition of accountability it no longer makes sense to put this question at the end of the planning methodology as it is in most public relations planning models. Therefore we have placed accountability at the heart of our strategy development methodology and link it directly to ambition.

Accountability is not a very popular subject in the communication field. This could have to do with time and money, but probably also with a fear of figures and lack of knowledge about measurement and evaluation. Although accountability is no longer an issue at most large corporations, the focus continues to be on showing output, and only output. To rectify the imbalance, the International Association of Measurement and Evaluation in Communication (AMEC) has developed an integrated evaluation framework that factors in the whole gamut of output, outtake, outcome, and impact.

HAVING AN AMBITION WITHOUT CONSTANTLY SHOWING THAT YOU ARE DOING THE RIGHT THINGS IN THE RIGHT WAY IS NO MORE THAN JUST A DREAM. THIS IS WHY ACCOUNTABILITY SHOULD BE PLACED AT THE HEART OF STRATEGY DEVELOPMENT METHODOLOGY AND LINKED DIRECTLY TO AMBITION.

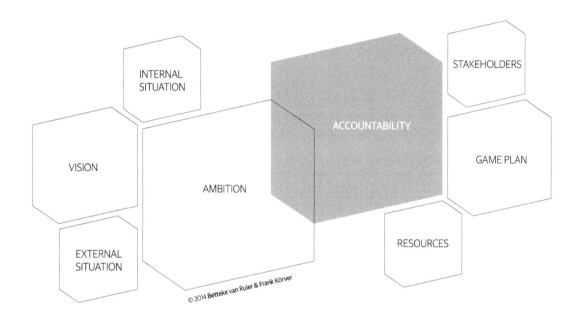

© 2014 Betteke van Ruler & Frank Körver

WHEN APPLYING THE COMMUNICATION STRATEGY FRAMEWORK, THERE ARE TWO QUESTIONS ABOUT ACCOUNTABILITY THAT YOU HAVE TO ANSWER:

1   Who is responsible for what, and how should they be responsible?
2   What are our KPIs and what method will we use to make them transparent?

⌐ Beware!
What you hold yourself accountable for is inextricably linked to your core values and your core task—in other words, to your ambition—as well as to your vision and game plan. That makes these four building blocks the core building blocks of the Communication Strategy Framework.

5 KICKSTARTERS

1   HOW DO YOU DEFINE ACCOUNTABILITY? DOES THAT DEFINITION MATCH TOP MANAGEMENT'S DEFINITION OF ACCOUNTABILITY?

2   WHAT DO YOU NEED TO KNOW, AT THE VERY LEAST, TO FUNDAMENTALLY STRENGTHEN YOUR ROLE IN THE ORGANIZATION?

3   WHAT DATA DO YOU NEED TO BE ABLE TO DO THE BEST POSSIBLE JOB?

4   WHAT METHODS AND DATA DO YOU CURRENTLY USE TO SHOW ACCOUNTABILITY? HOW VALID IS THIS INFORMATION?

5   WHICH DEPARTMENTS IN THE ORGANIZATION OR AT OTHER ORGANIZATIONS ARE FULLY ACCOUNTABLE? WHAT ARE THEY DOING RIGHT THAT YOU ADMIRE?

PROFESSIONAL ACCOUNTABILITY

Accountability is a subject about which much has been written. Many of those books and articles take it as a foregone conclusion that it is completely clear what the communication professional is supposed to do and be responsible for. That may hold true in some professions, but not in the field of communication. Start peeling back the layers of a generic label like "in charge of communication" and you'll quickly come up against a myriad of interpretations. For some it entails formal publicity across diverse media, for others marketing or sales support; for some it means control over every form of communication by and in the organization, for others it is about reputation, or about interaction with customers, and so on and so forth.

In practice, what the communication department or team oversees is dictated mainly by the organizational context and where it chooses to focus its energies. That of course differs from one organization to another. What one organization assigns to the domain of communication might be the domain of HR or strategy in another. In the end, who is doing what doesn't matter (however dubious the logic behind it), as long as it is obvious what the communication department is responsible for. After all, a department can only be accountable if it has clearly mapped out its responsibilities. That is why the Vision building block is so important.

Professional accountability is not about reiterating your ambition, but about translating your ambition into your day-to-day practice and activities. This lays the basis for your accountability. Imagine that you decide your core task is "strengthening our reputation." What does that make you responsible for, and in what way? Should you concentrate mainly on stakeholder management, or take the call center under your wing too, or is tackling corporate silence your biggest concern? Equally crucial, however, is specifying where your responsibilities end. Again, defining effective, management-backed communication standards in your vision is a big help.

MOUNTING AWARENESS OF SOCIAL ACCOUNTABILITY

Your own reflections on issues and solutions are increasingly challenged by societal moods and moral limitations. Put differently: whether a tactically smart move is also the ethically right choice. Social accountability, as this is called, concerns the values you adhere to in your work and what you contribute to society, and how. We all know that in the past communication has sometimes served as a powerful tool for achieving unethical or questionable ends, however short-lived. Communication can serve to mask or twist unpleasant messages, and as both the field and you as a professional mature, existential questions about how to handle this fact are inevitable. But this question also reflects the times we live in. Acting responsibly and scrupulously is necessary for trust, so this needs to be discussed explicitly in every communication department.

DECISIONAL AND PERFORMATIVE ACCOUNTABILITY

Accountability is not only about taking responsibility but also about answering for the things you do. The tool most commonly used to do that is performance indicators. The term "key performance indicator," KPI for short, was introduced by McKinsey in 1961 and in recent years has become part of the lingua franca of communication, too. Nevertheless, the idea of using KPIs has also met with considerable resistance, with some communication professionals fearful that it will reduce their work to a set of numeric targets. Is this the right way to approach communication? Won't KPIs kill creativity? Can we really capture communication in KPIs? Should we embrace this kind of standardization?

Not only do we believe KPIs are a good, managerial way to approach communication, we also think much of the debate surrounding these sorts of questions takes far too narrow a view of what these indicators are. Here, again, sailing offers a fitting metaphor. Imagine that your ambition is to sail from port A to port B as fast as possible. Your indicators, therefore, are the direction of the wind, the speed of the boat, the current, the weather forecast, your current position, and so forth. These indicators are aids that can help you to ascertain if you are indeed advancing from port A to port B, and they enable you to decide in time whether you need to adjust course—that is, change what you are doing—to get where you want to go. This is also known as decisional accountability.

Performative accountability, by contrast, is about showing your results. The AMEC has a useful program to help with this, which is available to download on its website (www.amecorg.com). Of course, communication does not produce straightforward results and it is always difficult to unravel what is in fact a result of your actions and what is due to other variables. Nonetheless, showing results is a good way to demonstrate your quick wins and successes, and that alone makes it worth delving into this in a little deeper.

Performance indicators are best understood as your objectives translated into empirical terms. They force you to commit to something and serve as guideposts to stay on track. This is precisely why the Communication Strategy Framework stresses the interdependence of your ambition and your KPIs, which in turn lay the basis for your game plan. Of course, it is entirely possible that once the time comes to start working out a game plan, you realize your KPIs are not wholly watertight. As in the other building blocks, this too is an iterative process.

DIFFERENT KINDS OF PERFORMANCE INDICATORS

There are several kinds of indicators you can use. Structure indicators yield information about the organizational conditions needed for performance. For instance, the position of the communication department within the organizational structure or its hierarchical or functional relationship to the communication director and management. You can also think of these as your conditions for success: "To achieve ambitions XYZ, we need..." Process indicators provide an indication of how processes are progressing. A good example of a process indicator is the amount of time it takes to answer a press query. But process indicators can also be about things like renewal or increased focus on results. Decision indicators help you to decide what your next action should be. For instance, the total number of people who are in favor of a specific action. Outcome indicators provide an indication of the actual results of your performance. This could be something like press coverage (both quantitative and qualitative!) or the impact of inhouse communication on employees' pride. Finally, there are predictive indicators. Examples of a predictive indicator are a good relationship with individual journalists or having access to management team meetings. They, too, can be seen as conditions for success.

Formulating indicators is no piece of cake. Dozens of management methods have been developed for the purpose and whole consultancy firms are devoted to it. KPIs make a concise statement of what needs to be measured and how it will be measured. Formulating them is a specialization unto itself, but with training and practice anyone can do it, and chances are there are people in your organization who can help. We furthermore advise limiting yourself to no more than ten KPIs, because otherwise you'll never get around to anything besides measuring. And as we all know: less is more.

CHOOSE THE RIGHT MEASUREMENT TOOLS

Apart from the challenge of formulating good KPIs, you also need an effective way to measure whether the results you wanted to achieve have indeed been achieved or are realistic. In practice, communication professionals tend to rely primarily on media analyses, force field analyses, and multi-stakeholder studies. This is fine,

BARCELONA PRINCIPLES: MEASURING YOUR RESULTS

Accountability is a hot topic in the communication field, which both the Swedish and English associations of communication professionals have been doing work on for years. Although the German DPRG association started later, it made up for it with pure German efficiency by partnering with the worldwide auditing association to develop an impressive system that has since become the standard in the German-speaking world (see www.communicationcontrolling.com for its English website).

AMEC has developed a set of basic principles for accountability that it introduced in 2010 and updated in 2017 and which are endorsed by a variety of international knowledge institutions and professional associations, including the Institute for Public Relations (IPR), the International Communications Consultancy Organization (ICCO), and the Public Relations Society of America (PRSA). These principles are known as the Barcelona Principles:

1   Goal setting and measurement are fundamental to communication and public relations.
2   Measuring communication outcomes is recommended versus only measuring outputs.
3   The effect on organizational performance can and should be measured where possible.
4   Measurement and evaluation require both qualitative and quantitative methods.
5   Advertising Value Equivalents (AVEs) are not the value of communications.
6   Social media can and should be measured consistently with other media channels.
7   Measurement and evaluation should be transparent, consistent, and valid.

Within the AMEC, current discussion is centered on two factors. First, the fact that measurement should concentrate not on media but on the basic ways in which an organization presents itself and the effects. It therefore conclusively rejects AVEs. Second, measurement should not only be used after the fact to establish whether results were achieved but (also) as a means to gather insights for the next action. This, effectively, is a shift from performative to decisional accountability, although the AMEC does not frame it in these terms.

⌐ See also:

http://amecorg.com/barcelona-principles-2-0/

however, be sure to choose a tool that aligns with your performance indicators. Say your main ambition is to regain employee trust and you have set KPIs for this challenge; clearly, a reputation study is probably not the best way to go. Incidentally, we feel that reputation research is overused as it is, but that's a different subject.

Another question is whether you should do qualitative or quantitative research. This choice is entirely up to you and, once again, it depends on what you want to know. Do you want to find out what stakeholders think about your organization? Then you may want to do a qualitative study that employs a narrative method to discover social stories. Do you want to know which publics hold a favorable view of your organization and which ones an unfavorable view? Then you will have to do a quantitative study. Basically, qualitative research helps you to discover the nature of an occurrence, while quantitative research tells you how prevalent it is. As a rule, be judicious with your surveys. People get bombarded with them as it is and in the end they often don't give you the information you were after anyway.

RELIABILITY

Ultimately, no matter what type of study or analysis you do, there is one inviolable golden rule: your method has to generate reliable information that actually tells you what you want to know. Eavesdropping on some coworkers' conversations over your lunch break and then concluding that "the organization" is negative about a board decision won't cut it. Conducting a reputation poll among the general public for a B2B company actually raises more questions than it answers. Neither are AVEs considered reliable in communication research (see the Barcelona Principles). But beyond that, we encourage you to get as creative as you want when choosing tools to measure your performance. Also, realize that in some cases communication is just a health factor, and the question you have to answer is whether you have contributed to preventing the destruction of value. This is not something you should be asking all too often, and of course you won't get a quantitative answer, but it can certainly help to shed some additional light on the communication department's value.

Finally, how you use your measurement tools is also important. Are they only intended to check whether you did something right after the fact? Or are they meant to or also able to justify your choices? In other words, which is your independent variable: your research or your actions? Which do you want to measure: your decisional or your performative accountability?

OVERPROMISING, UNDERDELIVERING

A common mistake that we see people make when defining performance indicators is that they get overly ambitious, propelled by either enthusiasm or hired consultants. From a near-term perspective the temptation is understandable because it shows that you are ambitious, and thinking big may well impress the management and score you points as a team. But if you don't manage to deliver on those promises, you have that much farther to fall. In consultancy terms this is called "overpromising, undelivering." Or for another well-worn adage: "If it sounds too good to be true, it probably is." In the end, the creation of sound performance indicators calls for a good balance between ambition and realism.

THE IMPORTANCE OF SOFT KPIs

Ideally, your KPIs measure not only hard but also soft factors. We all know that over-focusing on things like results and performance can detract from soft factors like team spirit, inspiration, and renewal. That soft side is every bit as important and, therefore, needs to be considered too. It also takes away a big concern that people have about KPIs. With both hard and soft indicators, what possible objection could there still be against using them?

In their book Beyond Performance Scott Keller and Colin Price (2011) underline the importance of leaders who understand how they can deliver performance today while also ensuring that their organizations stay fit for the future. This requires a focus on both "performance" and "health." The ideas of Keller and Price are particularly interesting when you relate them to KPIs. When developing KPIs one should not only focus on hard results, but also stay mindful of other softer factors that are good for the "health" of an enterprise, department, or team and may have no clear immediate benefit. According to Keller and Price health is the ability of an organization to align, execute, and renew itself (faster than the competition).

What does this imply for communication teams? Balancing the "hard" and the "soft" is essential. Although accountability is more often associated with hard factors, we believe it is as important to think about the "softer" dimensions. For example, ask yourselves: Are we doing enough to renew ourselves? What is the mindset of our staff? What is the mood within our team? Are we capable of going the extra mile in our execution?

10 DO'S AND DON'TS

1   Do revisit your vision and ask what you and your team should and can be responsible for in the current context, and how.

2   Do ask yourself: What do I really need to know to be able to do an outstanding job, and what information do I need to provide to play a consequential role in the organization?

3   Do make rigorous choices. This starts with mapping out your responsibilities. Then develop a limited set of KPIs and carefully select tools that will help you to measure if you are on course and whether you are attaining real results.

4   Do be realistic, both in mapping out your responsibilities and in defining your KPIs.

5   Don't confine yourself to performative accountability. Think of how you can boost your decisional accountability.

6   Do be meticulous in drawing up your KPIs, but also make sure it doesn't devolve into a never-ending project.

7   Do work together with all your teams to define KPIs. Also, have each team think about their own KPIs and revisit them periodically. A visual dashboard can help.

8   Don't choose your measurement tools based on "what we've already got" but based on "what we need"—and then make your choices.

9   Do find out which data is already being collected within the organization, for instance about individual stakeholder groups. Then consider how that data may be of use to you.

10 Do also think about the possible consequences of achieving—or not achieving—your KPIs. What will happen after you reach your targets? And what happens if you don't achieve them?

THIS BUILDING BLOCK DISCUSSED HOW YOU CAN BECOME ACCOUNTABLE. IN PRACTICE, THIS IS OFTEN LINKED TO QUANTITATIVE TARGETS. WE REJECT THIS AUTOMATIC ASSUMPTION AND BELIEVE ACCOUNTABILITY IS ALSO ABOUT QUALITATIVE AND SOFTER FACTORS. THE IMPORTANT THING IS THAT YOU SHOW WHAT YOU ARE DOING AND WHAT THE BENEFITS OF THOSE THINGS ARE. NOTHING MORE THAN THAT, BUT ALSO NOTHING LESS.

STRATEGIC CHOICES ARE THOSE THAT MAKE A DIFFERENCE FOR SUCCESS

COMMUNICATION STRATEGY

STRATEGIC CHOICES ARE THOSE THAT MAKE A DIFFERENCE FOR CORPO-
RATE SUCCESS—IN COMMUNICATIONS AS WELL AS IN OTHER AREAS LIKE
FINANCE, PRODUCTION, LOGISTICS, AND HUMAN RESOURCES.

IT IS A COMMON MISTAKE TO BASE SUCH CHOICES MAINLY ON CREATIVE
IDEAS, GUT FEELING OR PROFESSIONAL EXPERIENCE. AT THE SAME TIME,
LINEAR PLANNING ROUTINES KNOWN FROM PR AND ADVERTISING CAN-
NOT COPE WITH THE DYNAMICS AND SPEED OF TODAY'S WORLD. WE NEED
FRAMEWORKS AND MANAGEMENT TOOLS FOR CORPORATE COMMUNI-
CATIONS THAT GUIDE REFLECTION, SYSTEMATIZE INPUT FROM MULTIPLE
PERSPECTIVES, CAN BE FED WITH EMPIRICAL DATA AND BEST PRACTICES,
AND GUIDE DECISION-MAKING IN AN AGILE WAY. SUCH TOOLS ARE RARE IN
STRATEGIC COMMUNICATION.

IMPLEMENTING SUCH FRAMEWORKS FOR PLANNING, EXECUTING AND
MEASURING IS AN ATTRIBUTE OF COMMUNICATION EXCELLENCE.

Ansgar Zerfass, Ph.D.
Professor and Chair of Strategic Communication, University of Leipzig, Germany
Leadership Researcher, Global Communication Monitor series

BUILDING BLOCK
STAKEHOLDERS

The American R. Edward Freeman (1984), who developed the stakeholder theory, was the first person to suggest that there are many other stakeholders besides financiers—that is, shareholders—who deserve consideration. He defined a stakeholder as any individual or group of individuals that can influence the enterprise or can be influenced by the enterprise and as such have a stake in the organization's activities. Furthermore, Freeman proposed that stakeholders should be engaged in the creation of organizational policy. Others later detailed precisely who should be involved and how.

In the communication field we talk a lot about stakeholders—that is, the people who have a stake in our organization. Rarely, however, do we talk about the stakeholders in our communication strategy, even though there are quite a few people, groups, and organizations that are involved in one way or another in shaping and determining—and possibly hindering—a strategy's success. Perhaps most obvious is the target audience or public; that is, the "users" of a communication intervention. But there are many others whose support you need to gain, or that you at the very least have to stay in touch with. Therefore, we distinguish between stakeholders who are enablers and those who are partners.

Stakeholders can be either internal or external. A stakeholder can be another department, an internal unit, or specific individuals, groups, or even whole organizations separate from yours. It is becoming increasingly common for departments to team up both with other departments and with people and groups outside their organization to work on projects together. These are your partners. People are stepping out of their silos and walls are coming down, and the distinctions between who is internal and who is external are thus blurring. These days, those categories are no longer even considered all that relevant. Most important is that you can pinpoint which parties you need on board, internally or externally, to achieve your ambition.

IN THE COMMUNICATION FIELD WE TALK A LOT ABOUT THE STAKEHOLDERS IN THE ORGANIZATION, BUT WE RARELY TALK ABOUT THE STAKEHOLDERS IN OUR COMMUNICATION STRATEGY, OR WE FOCUS SOLELY ON OUR TARGET AUDIENCE.

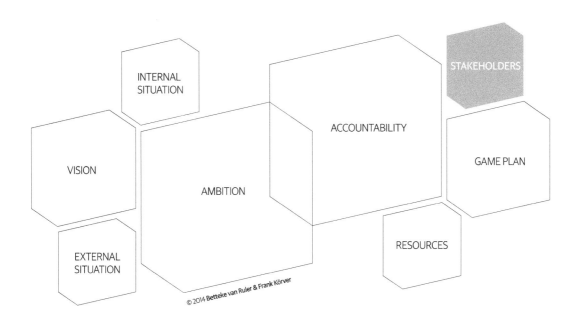

© 2014 Betteke van Ruler & Frank Körver

IN OUR CONCEPTION OF COMMUNICATION STRATEGY, STAKEHOLDERS CAN FALL INTO ONE OF TWO CATEGORIES:

1   The enablers: the individuals or groups whose commitment is crucial for your strategy to succeed.
2   The partners: the individuals or groups you have to work with and that have to actively contribute for you to achieve your communication strategy ambitions.

⌐ Beware!
The difficulty lies not so much in distinguishing who you need as enablers and who as partners, but in getting those people, departments, or organizations to accept their role, which is central to securing their commitment or cooperation.

5 KICKSTARTERS

1   WHO DO YOU NEED IN ORDER TO ACHIEVE YOUR AMBITIONS?

2   IN WHAT CAPACITY DO YOU NEED THOSE INDIVIDUALS OR GROUPS? HOW MUCH INFLUENCE DO THEY HOLD, AND TO WHAT EXTENT ARE THEY INTERESTED IN YOUR SUBJECT?

3   WHAT IS THE ROLE OF THE INDIVIDUALS OR GROUPS AT WHICH YOU WANT TO TARGET YOUR STRATEGY?

4   WHICH PARTIES DO YOU ROUTINELY COLLABORATE WITH, YET FAIL TO ACOMPLISH THE DESIRED RESULTS? WHICH PARTIES DO YOU NOT COLLABORATE WITH NOW, BUT WOULD LIKE TO?

5   HOW CAN YOU MAKE YOUR CEO OR MANAGER THE AMBASSADOR OF YOUR STRATEGY AND YOUR WORK?

WHO ARE YOUR ENABLERS?

How do you determine who you need on your side? When it comes to support for the organization as a whole, this list is fairly easy to draw up, and it has been, hundreds of times, in many a book and website. They include financiers, employees, members, labor unions, media, and so on and so forth. But what about support for a communication strategy? Furthermore, can you break down that list, and how? For instance, between the parties whose commitment you need for your strategy to succeed (the sponsors) and the parties you need to connect with because they can smooth the way for your plan, or conversely block it (the influencers)? Or based on whose commitment matters most?

By now it should be apparent that we believe communication plays an important strategic role at organizations, and also that, ideally, the head of the communication department reports directly to the head of the organization. If you ask us, the most important sponsor and influencer in any communication strategy is the CEO— or, if it is a strategy for a particular program or project—the person in charge of that program or project. Getting the backing of these people and convincing them of the value of what you are doing is your first step.

The next is figuring out who the other important stakeholders are. How? Quite simply by making a list. Start by asking yourself: Who are we actually doing this for? Who profits if our communication strategy works—who fails? Who are all the actors who can influence it, apart from our target audience—aka our "users." Who will be impacted, and how? Nine times out of ten, your list will include other functions in the organization such as the finance department, HR, marketing, and legal. Or you may have to turn to an NGO or to fellow professionals working on similar projects at other organizations. These types of stakeholders are different from the "target audiences" that your communication strategy is meant to activate to do something for or with you, but they are every bit as crucial.

Another thing that is useful to know is how much influence they could have, because that determines how you should approach them. Stakeholders are often categorized based on their degree of influence or power and their degree of importance. Depending on what you are looking for, this can result in various matrices. For lots of helpful examples, see www.stakeholdermap.com. This categorization by degree of influence and degree of importance then indicates what type of communication is needed per stakeholder. Clearly, the main individuals or groups for which your communication strategy is primarily intended—your target audience— should figure prominently in your matrix.

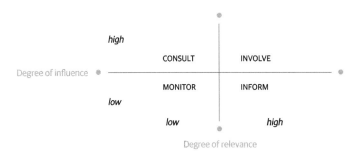

Figure 6. Example of a stakeholder analysis based on degree of influence and degree of relevance to the organization and the question how best to communicate with them

One of the most frequently cited theories on stakeholder analysis is that of Ronald K. Mitchell, Bradly R. Agle, and Donna J. Wood (1997), who argued that the most salient stakeholders for any organization are those that have the power to influence the organization, that are given legitimacy by other interested parties, and that can demonstrate the urgency of their claim. These attributes are equally valid for stakeholder theory as it applies to communication. Many others have elaborated this theory, such as Lynda Bourne (2006) in the Stakeholder Circle, which is designed for stakeholder management in projects and is also useful in the communication field.

STAKEHOLDER CIRCLE: POWER, URGENCY, INFLUENCE

Lynda Bourne is an Australian scholar who applied Mitchell, Agle, and Wood's stakeholder theory to projects and developed a model to rate the relative influence of various stakeholders and define their expectations. She refers to project stakeholders as "the sphere of influence and support on which a project depends for its very existence," and she, too, stresses the need to cultivate strong relationships with stakeholders. (See www.mosaicprojects. com.au.) The Stakeholder Circle identifies stakeholders according to power/proximity on the one hand and importance/urgency on the other, and then classifies them based on the direction of their influence (such as higher-ups in the hierarchy, coworkers, people in the same sphere of influence, externals). Instead of prescribing a fixed way of dealing with these various stakeholders, Bourne says this is something that has to be discussed on a regular basis within the project team.

WHO SHOULD YOU PARTNER WITH?

When thinking about this building block, we feel it is useful to distinguish between enablers and partners. Enablers are the people that most stakeholder analyses tend to focus on. Lately, however, there has been a growing awareness that another type of stakeholder should also be accounted for, namely the people or groups that you have to collaborate with to be able to achieve your goals. We call this latter category partners. For example, the audit department might be a good partner if you want to get issues surrounding the organization's reputation on the board agenda, while joining forces with HR could be a good idea if you are dealing with internal changes. The strategy department is your best ally if you want to arm yourself for the reputation opportunities and risks of an imminent merger or acquisition, whereas marketing can be a valuable partner for concerns about external image.

Who it is best to partner with is always a fairly subjective decision, and moreover one that hinges on all kinds of circumstantial factors such as whether the organization allows for such partnerships and whether the people in question get along. Obviously, however, your prospective partner has to want and believe in the partnership too. You could decide that it is crucial to form an alliance with the audit department, but if the audit department isn't interested because they see nothing in it for them, you will end up either empty-handed or very unhappily married. It is absolutely essential to cultivate good relationships with all disciplines you may need down the line. After all, you will never win anyone to your side if they don't know you, and everything we know about maintaining relationships in the outside world applies as much if not more so to those with other divisions or sister organizations.

Grant T. Savage and fellow researchers Timothy W. Nix, Carlton J. Whitehead, and John D. Blair (1991) proposed to group stakeholders based on the degree to which they can pose a threat to the organization and the degree to which they are willing to cooperate with it. It may seem odd to talk about potential partners in terms of threat levels, but it is valid nonetheless. Normally, our preference is to collaborate with departments, individuals, and organizations that will substantially enhance our chances of success, while keeping those that impede us (even if only in our minds) at the farthest possible distance. This is not the most sensible course of action, but it is what tends to happen. By identifying potential threats, however, you can question the logic of what your intuition is telling you.

Figure 7. Managing stakeholders based on the degree of threat and inclination to collaborate (Savage et al., 1991)

DEPENDENCIES

In modern planning theory, the process of thinking about ambitions tends to be linked automatically to thinking about possible factors that could aid or impede you in achieving them. On whom and on what are you dependent to succeed at your core tasks? Those dependencies can be internal or external. This does not mean they are inside or outside the organization but (as with SWOT) that they lie in or outside your sphere of influence. The idea of dependencies comes from scrum and, as defined in scrum methodology, refers to factors you must take into account and explicitly identify from the outset. That way, they cannot take you by surprise. Skipping this step makes your accountability dependent on others or on the situation and circumstances that unfold, without clarifying who or what beforehand. That's asking for trouble. Aptly, another term used for dependencies is success factors. One way to pinpoint your dependencies or success factors is to think about how different scenarios could play out and what might get in the way.

Of course, it is impossible to map out every single contingency. But that's okay. Like a scrum project plan, the Communication Strategy Framework is not meant to be a fixed blueprint. As with any planning model, it has to be continually readjusted. Dependences, too, can be revisited and recalibrated—at every planning meeting if necessary—providing a valuable constant reminder that it is not up to you alone to get things done, but that you are dependent on other people and circumstances. The individuals and groups that you have to depend on fall under the Stakeholders building block. The resources you have to depend on fall under the Resources building block.

It all depends on why someone (or a department or an organization) should partner with you. Often, it is because not doing so forms a threat to their success as well. In other words, there has to be payoff for them, too. Sometimes you have to help your prospective partner a little by spelling out what they will gain. Though this is time-consuming, in the end you will reap the rewards.

GIVE AND TAKE

Savage subsequently tackled the question of what role stakeholders have to be able to play to make them good partners. In a 2011 coauthored article he argued that whereas stakeholder theory always focuses on the organization, collaboration should center on nurturing a relationship, and these two things can be at odds with each other. In other words, you have to shift focus away from the organization and aim it more specifically at that relationship. Moreover, because a partnership is about collectivity and joining forces—even if the partners have diverging or even conflicting interests—the objectives of the partnership will be dictated by that collectivity. That makes this relationship fundamentally different to that with the enablers we discussed earlier.

Developing a partnership, Savage et al. (2011) go on to say, demands a network perspective, which lets you delineate the precise position that everybody occupies in your network of relationships. For effective collaboration, two things are vital. First, there have to be symmetrical interests and benefits. There have to be benefits for both parties and you have to clearly articulate the joint interest. A successful partnership requires that all partners feel themselves to be dependent on one another and see an advantage to working together. They have to agree on a shared definition of the matter at hand, to organize a framework in which to structure their collaboration, to learn to trust one another, and to forge a shared identity and thus the solidarity that will enable them to carry out their activities together. Second, the partnership has to preserve the integrity of each participant. Relationships in which one or both parties feel straitjacketed are not likely to thrive.

Partnership is not a zero-sum game. If only one party benefits, it is not a partnership. Collaboration theory states that value has to be created for both parties, and that can only happen if both sides put their trust in the other, respect the other, more or less agree on the essentials, and communicate openly and honestly with one another. We all know that it "take two to tango." For a partnership to work, both parties have to be willing and able to embark on the relationship. And that is precisely what makes partnerships so tricky.

10 DO'S AND DON'TS

1   Do be aware that your target audience is just one of the many stakeholders in your success, though obviously their commitment is crucial.

2   Do keep a list of "important players" and make sure it is always up to date.

3   Do put an effort into matters that, though perhaps not directly relevant to your work, could aid in expanding your network inside and outside the organization.

4   Don't only think in terms of what potential partners can offer you, be clear about what you have to offer them.

5   Do go into every partnership striving to create a win-win situation and also be clear about what each partner stands to gain from the relationship. Be transparent with one another.

6   Don't confine yourself to only inhouse stakeholders; also cultivate good relationships with external parties such as journalists, scientists, consultancies, research agencies, and so on.

7   Don't approach relationships from only a short-term perspective; always keep an eye to the long term as well.

8   Do invest the necessary time in maintaining ties with your stakeholders, realizing that this investment will be considerable. And don't let yourself get sidetracked from this by issues of fleeting relevance.

9   Do be selective. You cannot have an equally strong relationship with everyone, nor do you need to.

10 Do realize that the playing field is constantly changing. Stay alert, keep your finger on the pulse, and remember that not only who your stakeholders are may change, but stakeholders themselves may change their positions.

THIS BUILDING BLOCK FOCUSED ON WHO YOUR STAKEHOLDERS ARE. WE DISTINGUISH BETWEEN ENABLERS, WHO NEED TO COMMIT TO YOUR STRATEGY, AND PARTNERS. HOW YOU DEAL WITH THESE TWO TYPES OF STAKEHOLDERS IS THE FOCUS OF THIS BUILDING BLOCK.

STRATEGIC MANAGEMENT OF PUBLIC RELATIONS IS THE MOST IMPORTANT WAY OF OVERCOMING ITS MARGINALIZATION

LARISSA GRUNIG ON COMMUNICATION STRATEGY

COMMUNICATION STRATEGY

WHATEVER WE CALL IT—PUBLIC RELATIONS, PUBLIC AFFAIRS, OR COMMUNICATION—OUR CHOSEN FIELD IS VITAL TO ORGANIZATIONAL SUCCESS.

WHY IS IT, THEN, THAT THE PUBLIC RELATIONS FUNCTION IS SO OFTEN MARGINALIZED? IN A NUTSHELL: LACK OF STRATEGIC THINKING AND PLANNING. IN MY VIEW, THE ROLE OF STRATEGIC MANAGEMENT OF PUBLIC RELATIONS IS THE SINGLE MOST IMPORTANT WAY OF OVERCOMING ITS MARGINALIZATION. AND THAT, IN TURN, IS CRITICALLY IMPORTANT IN HELPING TAKE OUR ROLE FROM SIMPLY A MOUTHPIECE TO BECOMING THE EYES AND EARS OF THE ORGANIZATION. WHEN WE DO THAT, AS STRATEGIC MANAGERS, WE CAN REPRESENT THE LEGITIMATE CONCERNS OF OUR PUBLICS—INTERNAL AND EXTERNAL.

BY COMMUNICATING AND HELPING DEVELOP RELATIONSHIPS WITH ACTIVE PUBLICS, WE INCREASE THE LIKELIHOOD OF DESIRABLE COMMUNICATION EFFECTS. IN MY EXPERIENCE, THERE IS A REAL NEED FOR SUCH ETHICAL AND KNOWLEDGEABLE COMMUNICATORS ALL AROUND THE WORLD.

Larissa Grunig, Ph.D.
Professor emerita in public relations
University of Maryland, United States of America

BUILDING BLOCK
RESOURCES

Resources usually refer to people and money. By people we mean all the players that you want to engage in your communication strategy and their specific competences. First and foremost, these are your inhouse communication professionals and any additional assistance you hire in. With all the reorganizations of recent years, many communication teams have been left considerably depleted. Ironically, during that time demand for communication's added value has only increased and continues to do so. The question, to put it boldly, is how you can do more with less. This is no small challenge, nor is there a simple solution, even if a plethora of quotes and articles would like to convince you otherwise.

For many communication departments, the answer to the question of how to do more with less has come in the form of an alternative departmental structure. Some have rigorously pruned their tasks and functions. Others have consolidated their main activities and now work with independent contractors when and as needed. Besides slimming down departments, all the reorganizations and cuts have also sparked a fundamental discussion about which people are needed inhouse and which ones can be hired in. For the record, we are not fans of cost cutting that skims off a little bit across the board, because that sidesteps fundamental and necessary choices.

These days we are all increasingly aware of the fact that everybody in the organization communicates and that communication strategies have to actively take this into account. Given all these factors, it makes sense that you often need other people in the organization—managers, experts, and other departments—to play a part in communication. And we haven't even talked about the other resource yet: money. Without money, your strategy will almost certainly be dead in the water. Getting the money you want is usually a matter of good negotiating skills and sometimes of dogged persistence. Crucially, this is an area where you can cash in on a good relationship with the CEO and management that we discussed in the Stakeholders building block.

WHERE THE STAKEHOLDERS BUILDING BLOCK WAS ABOUT DESCRIBING WHO YOU
HAVE TO DEPEND ON FOR YOUR STRATEGY TO BE A SUCCESS, THE RESOURCES
BUILDING BLOCK IS ABOUT DESCRIBING WHO HAS TO IMPLEMENT THE STRATEGY,
WHICH COMPETENCES ARE REQUIRED, AND HOW MUCH MONEY YOU NEED.

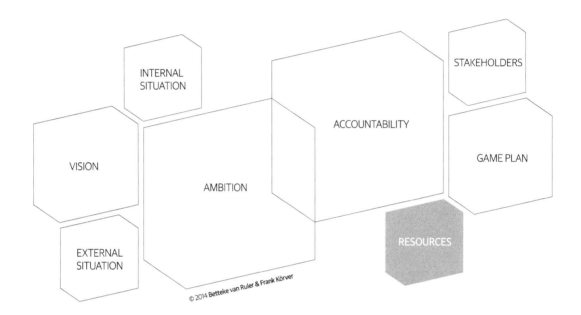

© 2014 Betteke van Ruler & Frank Körver

THIS BUILDING BLOCK CENTERS ON TWO QUESTIONS:

1 Which people with what competences do you need to achieve your ambitions?
2 What size and what type of a budget do you need?

⌐ Beware!
*It is sad but true that in many organizations the communication budget is not
open for negotiation. You have to make do with the same amount as last year, or
possibly even less. End of discussion. It takes some ingenuity and the right kind of
relationships to contrive to obtain what you really need.*

5 KICKSTARTERS

1   AT WHAT LEVEL DOES YOUR DEPARTMENT HAVE TO EXCEL—
    STRATEGIC, MANAGEMENT, OPERATIONAL—IN ORDER TO ACHIEVE ITS
    AMBITIONS? DO YOU HAVE THE RIGHT COMPETENCES ON BOARD?

2   WHICH COMPETENCES DO YOU AS AN EXPERT JUDGE OTHERS IN THE
    ORGANIZATION NEED TO CONTRIBUTE TO YOUR COMMUNICATION
    STRATEGY?

3   ARE YOUR COMMUNICATION PROFESSIONALS MAINLY FOCUSED ON
    DELIVERING RESULTS OR ARE THEY ALSO MASTERS OF NETWORKING
    AND BUILDING RELATIONSHIPS? WHAT COULD BE IMPROVED?

4   HOW WOULD YOU CHARACTERIZE THE DESIRED AND THE ACTUAL
    OVERALL MINDSET OF YOUR COMMUNICATION PROFESSIONALS? AND
    OF OTHER PEOPLE IN THE ORGANIZATION?

5   IN WHAT TERMS DO INHOUSE CUSTOMERS TEND TO DESCRIBE THE
    COMMUNICATION STAFF? DOES THIS COINCIDE WITH YOUR DESIRED
    IMAGE?

KEY COMPETENCES

The term competence refers to the specialist knowledge, understanding, skills, and attitudes needed to perform a given task. We prefer to use the word "expert." An expert is someone with the ability to do the right thing in the right way at the right time. A distinction is often made here between routine expertise and adaptive expertise (see, for example, Holyoak, 1991). Routine experts can quickly and accurately solve problems through application of learned procedures, while adaptive experts are consistently able to come up with new procedures. Routine expertise is acquired by studying procedures developed by experienced experts. Adaptive expertise requires a broad base of applicable knowledge from which you can mold solutions as the situation requires.

Keeping routine knowledge up to date is a matter of training. Adaptive knowledge is developed by reading books and specialist journals, investigating how fellow practitioners do things, taking courses, and going to seminars. A large share of adaptive knowledge, moreover, qualifies as tacit knowledge. This is knowledge that cannot be learned or obtained from books, but that is internalized by people, and to unlock it in your team, you have to encourage dialogue about how things have been done in the past and how you want to do them in the future. In communication, adaptive expertise is becoming increasingly important, and so too, therefore, is the need for ongoing education, reflection, and discussion.

In the 1970s the sociologists H. Jamous and B. Peloille (1970) proposed that occupational work could be understood as a combination of technically definable activity and the formation of professional judgment. They termed these two dimensions "technicality" and "indeterminacy." Technicality consists in the knowledge and skills prescribed by existing rules. Indeterminacy, by contrast, concerns whether there are continuously changing or new questions or problems that cannot be solved through the application of existing rules and procedures and which require the capability to draw on general knowledge. We like to call this conceptual creativity.

Both types of tasks are encountered in the field of communication, but these days a very perceptible shift is taking place away from technicality and toward indeterminacy. Even the composition of a text relies more on conceptual creativity. You could go so far as to say that technicality is on its way to becoming a dissatisfier; you need it in your arsenal, but it won't win the war. Indeterminacy is where you can really add value. The ECOPSI research project (Tench, 2015) shows that the field is indeed moving from the mostly operational and routine into the more managerial and strategic, and that strategic competences are seen as key to adding real value. Strategic insight is therefore becoming ever more important. This calls for all the more conceptual creativity, the ability to think outside the box and to improvise, and to do that strategically, which means you need not only knowledge, but also—and perhaps even more so—a specific attitude.

THE RIGHT ATTITUDE

David Maister has written many books about professionals, and in them he argues that attitude is the foundation of professionalism. Knowledge, he emphasizes, can be taught; attitude has to be cultivated and is demonstrated in dedication, passion, and enthusiasm. Less important than what a professional knows is what he or she thinks, how they "play the game." Knowledge about your field is clearly a requisite and your foundation, but the secret of a good practitioner is that they can tap into their creativity and enthusiasm and are able to demonstrate their absolute dedication.

As the Public Relations Society of America (PRSA) says on its website, "although you might think that you only deal with media and publics, you also need the ability to get along well with others. You must be persuasive and able to negotiate. In addition, as a PR specialist, you will have to coordinate your actions with the actions of others, including your colleagues." In other words, don't wait for your turn, take it. To succeed in this field, you have to be an enterprising self-starter.

According to Dutch business and marketing consultant and guru Goos Geursen, professionals should be doing more of what we'll translate as "thacting" (in his book *Als de leuning beweegt*, or "When the support moves"; his term is doenken). The general assumption is that we think first and then act, premised on the idea that if we have done a good job of thinking something through, all that is left is to implement it. Geursen argues that letting the two run together—hence, thacting— leads to better decisions. But this idea is not entirely new. Much longer ago, in his book *The Reflective Practitioner,* Donald Schön (1983) wrote that in the process of any task you have to constantly reflect on whether you are doing it well, and then on whether you are reflecting well. It should be evident that we are very much in favor of "thacting," but it does require guideposts to evaluate whether you are "thacting" well. The Communication Strategy Framework provides the necessary guidance.

COMMUNICATION IS TEAMWORK

Teamwork is incredibly important. Fortunately, it is also increasingly getting the attention it deserves. Most departments now place as big a focus on team composition and team development as on professional expertise. One widely used team development model is that introduced by Bruce W. Tuckman in 1965, which distinguishes the stages of forming, storming, norming, performing, and adjourning. This was also the basis of the maturity model that many team development specialists use today.

A concept we really like is "teaming." Harvard Business School professor Amy C. Edmondson has done extensive research in this field and emphasizes the importance of "big teaming," referring to intense collaboration between professions and even industries with completely different mindsets. Edmondson (2012) believes that projects increasingly require information and that managers are dependent on all kinds of specialists to make decisions and get work done. "To excel in a complex and uncertain business environment, people need to work together in new and unpredictable ways. That's why successful teaming starts with an embrace of the unknown and a commitment to learning that drives employees to absorb, and sometimes create, new knowledge while executing" (p. 80).

An essential concept when talking about teamwork is leadership. Often, this is considered from the classical perspective of "who will direct the team?" Though this question is certainly valid, these days teams are also expected to be able to show shared leadership. The idea of self-organizing teams is an interesting concept that we think deserves to be utilized more in the communication field. Self-organization keys in to the trend to rely less on monitoring and management and to maximize people's individual potential. Deciding how and how much to work in self-organizing teams naturally depends on the context. What is certain, however, is that a team which has its sights set on a shared objective and shared performance and which makes shared agreements about those things will likely work much more efficiently and effectively than a classical team that waits for the "leader" to hand out tasks and instructions. One prerequisite is that the team has to possess a high level of maturity. Incidentally, this is also why more and more experts now are warning against rewarding team members individually; only by rewarding them as a group can you foster the right team spirit.

BUDGETING

Many organizations have standard procedures for budgeting, but this mostly concerns what to record and how, or to which budget things like computers or inventory should be attached. Far more important, however, is the question what kind of budget you need, or are allocated, and what that amount is based on.

METHODS FOR BUDGETING

There is not a great deal of information available in the communication field about what to base your budget on. Fortunately, we can look to marketing and to public relations planning systems, for instance, for detailed discussions of available methods (see, for example, Smith, 2013). The options they describe boil down to essentially the same thing. We sum them up.

The percentage of revenue method: The communication department is allocated a percentage of the organization's anticipated revenue. The advantage of this method is that it is straightforward and simple; the downside is that it does not factor in the communication strategy's substantive requirements. It is a method used in marketing, but we have never yet seen it used in communication. There is one related to it in our field, however, in which the better the results and more favorable the economic climate, the bigger the chance of a larger budget. Somewhat scarier is the method premised on estimated sales growth, about which we have serious doubts.

The affordability method: This is what Smith calls the "all-you-can-afford-method"; basically, whatever money is left over after deduction of all the organization's other costs is allocated to the communication department. We refuse to believe that any self-respecting organization would employ this method, especially since there is no benefit that we can see. Fortunately, we have yet to find this method in use in any communication department.

The parity method: In the advertising industry it is customary to look at what competitors, most notably the market leader, are spending on campaigns. Some organizations even conduct benchmarks to find out how large a budget or team comparable communication departments have. Provided you compare on the right dimensions, this can make sense. It certainly can be instructive, though primarily to find out why they spend what they spend. There can be all kinds of reasons why one organization spends more or less on this than another that has similar objectives.

The product life cycle method: This is a method widely used in the advertising industry that may also be fruitful for other segments of communication. If you are thinking of doing something totally new, you will need a hefty communication budget. If you are consolidating, you can do with less. To this, we would add that if you are in the public eye, you need more than if your organization is operating on the relative sidelines. If you are in the midst of a big transition, you will also need more.

The cost-benefit method: This method assumes that you can reliably anticipate the effect of your strategy and draw up your budget based on that. Its application is limited mostly to small projects, like an open house, and can aid in judging whether it would be useful to do something, and to evaluate afterward if it indeed was. But its usefulness for communication strategy seems slim.

The objective-based method: Here, the communication department gets a budget based on the ambitions to which the organization has committed, also called task-based budgeting. Though it requires a clear plan and lots of negotiation, the objective-based method is generally viewed as the only genuinely sound method. We agree.

Some organizations draw up a budget once annually and then it's case closed until next year. You could wonder if this is really the most sensible approach. Another that seems to be getting more popular is to give the department a basic budget to cover its fixed costs (preferably using the objective-based method) and then have it draw up separate budgets for each project requiring its expertise. One big advantage of this method is that it automatically secures commitment from others in the organization that want a particular communication issue dealt with, because they have to pay. A drawback is that members of the department then also have to record and haggle over the time investment as you would at an independent agency, which is something few people enjoy.

TIPS FOR PREPARING A COMMUNICATION BUDGET
Practice shows what works and what doesn't when developing
communication budgets:

- Be explicit about how you used your budget during the prior year, what it
  did and did not deliver, and what this signifies for next year's budget.

- Avoid nitpicking over details. Your discussions should focus on the big
  picture. You could do a few rough itemizations (people, campaigns, channels, etc.) giving a breakdown of how you intend to spend your budget.

- Build in flexibility by stressing that the budget will be reviewed in the
  event of an increase in demand (due to crises or issues, for instance).
  Using estimates can also provide a buffer.

- Ensure that someone is always monitoring the budget and make it a
  fixed part of his or her duties.

- You want to have a strong starting position for next year's budget
  negotiations, so be good and stick faithfully to the budget cycle.

10 DO'S AND DON'TS

1   Do make certain that job descriptions are always up to date; amend them if your ambitions change.

2   Do strike a good balance between "performance" and "health" in how you manage your professionals and continue to carefully monitor both.

3   Do set aside time at every management meeting to discuss the health and performance of your professionals.

4   Do know who the underperformers are and whose talents to cherish; don't forget to make real efforts to bind and inspire talented people.

5   Do set the bar high, but also be clear about your actual expectations. Professionals have the right to know on what they are being judged.

6   Do engage internal customers in the assessment of your professionals in order to get the whole picture.

7   Don't shy away from unpopular decisions and don't put off showing underperformers the door.

8   Do fight for your budget: don't simply cave in to cuts but stand up for the ambitions you have set.

9   Do stay in control of your finances and avoid nasty surprises that force you to pull out all the stops toward the end of the year.

10 Do, when budget cuts are on the way, prepare a thorough analysis of how you could still achieve your desired impact. Only curb your ambitions if there is no other option.

THE RESOURCES BUILDING BLOCK CENTERS ON PEOPLE AND MONEY. YOU MAY HAVE BIG AMBITIONS, BUT YOU ALSO HAVE TO BE REALISTIC. INCREASINGLY, OR-GANIZATIONS ARE SEEKING TO DO MORE WITH LESS. YOU CAN ONLY DO THAT IF YOU MAKE DECISIVE CHOICES AND KNOW EXACTLY WHICH COMPETENCES YOU NEED TO ACHIEVE YOUR AMBITIONS, AND EVEN THEN, YOU OFTEN HAVE TO BE VERY PERSISTENT TO GET THE FUNDS YOU REQUIRE.

AN AGILE
STRATEGIC MODEL
IS AN IMPERATIVE
GUIDE TO TACKLE
COMPLEXITY

ÁNGELES MORENO **ON COMMUNICATION STRATEGY**

COMMUNICATION
STRATEGY

SOMETHING DIFFICULT, JUDGING BY WHAT IS SEEN IN THE CLASSROOM AND WORKING PRACTICE, IS THE CORRECT WRITING OF AN OBJECTIVE.

IF WE THINK ABOUT AN INTRINSIC INGREDIENT THAT ACTS AS AN ANCHOR IN EVERY SECTION OF THE STRATEGIC MODEL, THESE ARE THE KEY OBJECTIVES. THE MODEL IS THE TREE, BUT THE OBJECTIVES ARE THE SEEDS INSIDE THE APPLE'S CORE; WHICH CONTAIN THE VERY ESSENCE OF THE PRESENT AND THE ORIGIN OF THE FUTURE. A WELL-DEFINED OBJECTIVE REQUIRES A DEEP KNOWLEDGE ABOUT THE ENVIRONMENT, STAKEHOLDERS, INFLUENCE, EFFECTS OF COMMUNICATIONS AND ALSO THE AIMS, THE CULTURE, THE MANAGEMENT AND ACCOUNTABLE PROCESSES OF A GIVEN ORGANIZATION.

THUS, AN AGILE STRATEGIC MODEL IS AN IMPERATIVE GUIDE FOR PRACTITIO- NERS TO TACKLE THE ENTIRE COMPLEXITY OF A MORE AND MORE DISRUPTIVE PRESENT. OBJECTIVES ARE THE SEEDS INSIDE THE TIME CORE.

Ángeles Moreno, Ph.D.
Professor of public relations
TU Universidad Rey Juan Carlos, Spain
Director of the Latin America Communication Monitor

BUILDING BLOCK
GAME PLAN

In the daily practice of many businesses, a game plan usually takes the shape of an operational plan of action with a timeline and a budget. We mean something different. In the Communication Strategy Framework, the Game Plan building block consists of the most important choices that will guide your operational activities. If you make the wrong choices at this stage, they will have immediate negative effects. Chances are, not only will you tackle the wrong things, you also will not achieve the impact you envisioned. Your aim, once again, is to create focus.

This can only be achieved if there is a results-based culture among the people doing the actual work. Only then can you create focus. In things such as channels, target audiences, messages, obtainable results; and the focus need to be concrete.

The Game Plan building block is where you specify what you want to do in concrete terms. It is where you formulate how you will effectuate your strategy. The other building blocks compelled you to make important choices; now the time has come to transpose those choices into specific tactics. With whom do you intend to communicate? What specific content do you need to do that, and which people will you target, and through which channels? And, most importantly, how are you going to do this? These questions are about your operational strategy. Two things are crucial here: your focus on the content and your focus on "the other"—whether it be a customer, a target audience, a segment of the public or other specific group, a B2B partner, or society at large. Though the role these groups play differs for every organization, the common denominator is that "the other" has to stay front and center in your strategic game plan at all times. The core question you should be asking is: In what way and using which content can we best connect with "the other"?

IN THE DAILY PRACTICE OF MANY BUSINESSES, A GAME PLAN USUALLY TAKES THE SHAPE OF AN OPERATIONAL PLAN OF ACTION WITH A TIMELINE AND A DETAILED BUDGET. WE MEAN SOMETHING DIFFERENT. THE GAME PLAN BUILDING BLOCK IS ABOUT YOUR OPERATIONAL STRATEGY AND YOUR SPECIFIC PRIORITIES.

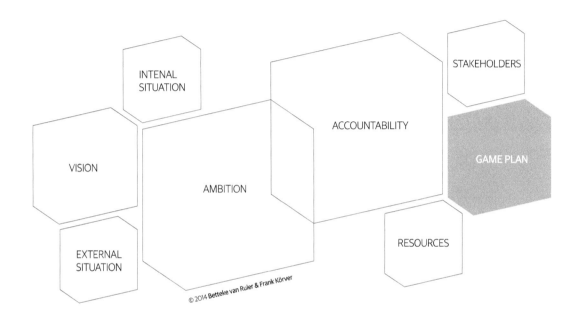

© 2014 Betteke van Ruler & Frank Körver

TWO COMPETENTS ARE IMPORTANT IN THE GAME PLAN BUILDING BLOCK:

1   Your operational strategy: Who do you want to do what, or with whom do you want to build relationships, and how will you do so?
2   Overall planning schedule and priorities: What will you do first, and what can wait until later?

⌐ Beware!
Everything you formulated in the other building blocks has to lead to decisive and practical, concrete choices in this building block. If your choices don't align, your strategy will not be congruent, and you will have to revisit the other building blocks.

5 KICKSTARTERS

1   TAKE A LOOK AT YOUR CURRENT PROGRAMS AND PROJECTS. HOW DO THEY FIT INTO YOUR AMBITIONS?

2   TO WHAT EXTENT ARE YOU LED BY HYPE AND HEADLINES, AND HOW COULD YOU PREVENT THAT IN THE FUTURE?

3   HOW CAN YOU TRANSLATE YOUR AMBITIONS INTO PRACTICAL OPERATIONAL STRATEGIES AND COMMUNICATION PRIORITIES?

4   WHAT WILL BE YOUR MAIN FLAGSHIP PROJECTS THIS YEAR OR IN THIS ENDEAVOR? WHICH PROJECTS WILL REALLY SHOWCASE YOUR ADDED VALUE?

5   HOW OFTEN DO YOU CONSULT WITH COWORKERS ON WHAT HAS TO BE DONE FIRST AND WHAT CAN WAIT UNTIL LATER?

WHAT ARE WE ACTUALLY GOING TO DO?

In *The Connected Company,* David Gray and Thomas van der Wal (2012) observe that "To keep pace with today's connected customers, your company must become a connected company." Their central thesis is that it is vital for organizations to stay engaged with their employees, customers, and stakeholders. But to do that, you have to know who you want to engage with and why and decide which content you want to use to feed that relationship. What dialogues do you want to have? What do you want to get across? What is your story? What kind of content are you going to produce? And for or with whom? How will you ensure your content aligns with what "the other" wants to hear? Or, instead, do you want to produce new content together? How will you keep control, and with whom and how will you communicate? All these questions come together in your operational strategy. Modern-day organizations are no longer machines to be monitored but dynamic systems that can (and must) learn and stay agile, and the same goes for communication departments. That said, you always need to have some sort of blueprint for what you want to do.

We have already said that a strategy is the road you choose to travel to your destination. When you have completed the Communication Strategy Framework, you will have set out your strategy. Within that Framework, this building block centers on the all-important question: What is our definitive game plan? Without an operational strategy, your department will never be able to make the difference, nor will anyone else in the organization take you seriously. In fact, this is the biggest concern within many organizations. With the Framework as your guide, you can formulate arguments to validate the game plan you choose.

Many roads lead to Rome, and at times a detour can be a smart option if it means you can avoid certain obstacles along the way. Ever heard of the "two steps forward, one step back" strategy? It's an approach that gets cited a lot in practice, much like the "you can't win if you don't play" strategy, or the "divide and conquer" or "zero-tolerance" strategies. There are as many different names for operational strategies as there are people to think them up.

One operational strategy that is backed up by hard scientific evidence is the "stealing thunder" strategy, which is where you break sensitive news about yourself first before someone else does. That way, you stay in control. This operational strategy often governs crisis communication. In health communication, a big question recently has been whether a fear-based strategy or a reward-based strategy is more effective

THE COMMUNICATION GRID

Communication can be seen as the process by which people try to relate to others by expressing their thoughts and feelings. The question is what form of communication is the most effective. This is where the Communication Grid can help. The grid differentiates between four operational strategies, which are distinguished by fundamental choices about whether the communication should be one-way or two-way and whether it is informational in purpose, or persuasive.

There is a tendency in our field to frown on the concept of one-way communication as such, but that is because to only send a message is never enough; you also have to check what the recipient does with it. For that reason, we prefer to talk about "controlled one-way communication."

Figure 8. The Communication Grid of tactics (van Ruler, 2004)

A one-way strategy requires a clear message, whereas a two-way strategy is focused on reaching a shared perspective on something. For the former, the organization has to have an opinion already formed; for the latter, it has to be open to forming an opinion in concert with others. A one-way strategy hinges on the other being receptive to absorbing information or to being persuaded; in a two-way strategy the other has to have formed an opinion on the subject under discussion but be willing to re-examine it. The latter is what we also call an aware or active public.

(the latter seems to be winning out). A strategy widely used in marketing is the early adopter strategy, based on Everett M. Rogers' (1995) diffusion of innovations theory. Persuasion is the standard strategy in marketing communication, and in public relations and corporate communication dialogue strategy is the current favorite.

GUIDELINES FOR IMPLEMENTATION

In practice, the chosen operational strategy is by no means always stated. Sometimes, the elaboration itself is regarded as the operational strategy, which is fleshed out in the interaction with stakeholders. This fits with the current thinking about strategy as something that takes shape as you go along. In that case, your operational strategy is a co-creation strategy or an incremental strategy. The first thing you need to do in this phase, therefore, is to think about the kind of planning method you want to use for your implementation. Do you like to follow a detailed series of steps, or do you prefer to go the agile route and define your content and "the other" along the way?

A second important question is whether different operational strategies are needed for internal versus external communication, and if you should diversify it for the various categories of people you want to communicate with. Will you target managers differently than employees, or teens differently than seniors?
The prevailing tendency now is not to differentiate between internal and external. Briefly, it was popular to distinguish between types of media—choosing one strategy for social media and another for all the rest—but that trend is over, according to the trade journals. Currently, it is about any-line. Increasingly, it is being debated whether adapting messages and tactics to different target audiences really serves a purpose. That's because customers are never only customers. They might also be a member of an activist group, or the neighbor of one of your employees, or a shareholder—or even all three. In that case, what segmentation criteria can you apply?

A third key question is how the operational strategy fits with the inhouse style of communication (see the Internal Situation building block). A strategy directed at two-way communication, such as a dialogue strategy, tends to misfire in rigidly hierarchical organizations that are unaccustomed to talking with their stakeholders. A conversational strategy aimed at making communication more personal will not work in an organization that is normally cool and formal in its communications. If you want to do either of these anyway, you will have to address things inside the organization first.

At this stage, your objective is to formulate some basic criteria that your daily activities have to fulfill. Here, just as in all the other building blocks, it is crucial to touch base with the other functions in your organization. Maybe they are already working with agile planning methods: could that be useful for you, too? Or if marketing has already jumped on the "conversational" bandwagon, you can join them.

As a final tip, we recommend reading *The Story of Purpose* by Joey Reiman (2013), who argues that organizations should be much more driven to take a position on issues than they do now ("from brand to stand"). Like him, we believe in the power of taking a clear stand and sending a clear message.

SET PRIORITIES
Sometimes it can be tempting to try to tackle everything all at once, but rarely is that the wisest course. Setting priorities means making choices. What has to be done first? What can wait until later? In communication, there is a tradition of simply taking to hand whatever needs doing, without thinking much about strategy. Little wonder then that the art of prioritizing still tends to elude us. Often, it is much easier to just

---

THE IMPORTANCE OF FLAGSHIP PROJECTS
Make sure that your game plan does not end up being nothing more than an arbitrary list of activities. This is not to say your plan should not include activities—on the contrary, in many contexts, specifying actions make good sense. However, you have to be selective, and the activities you carry out have to exemplify the strategic choices you make.

It can also be a good idea to define so-called flagship projects: roughly five projects or activities that you deem to be the most important of all; projects that others will also recognize as being vital or leading, and that will make a real impact.

Designating flagship projects will make your game plan come to life, thus enabling you to show how your strategy will be put into practice. But equally, they represent a promise, making a statement about the projects and activities through which you intend to make the difference in the time ahead. For instance, whereas preparing an annual report will seldom be an activity that makes the difference, that big cultural program you have in the pipeline or the publicity offensive around the new CEO could make an excellent flagship project.

work your way through an arbitrary list of activities than to rank or differentiate them based on a set of clear strategic priorities. Yet, as a professional, this is an art you need to master.

This is where Eisenhower's Urgent/Important Principle comes in. In a 1954 speech former U.S. president Dwight D. Eisenhower, visiting the campus of Northwestern University for the Second Assembly of the World Council of Churches, said: "I have two kinds of problems, the urgent and the important. The urgent are not important, and the important are never urgent." This "Eisenhower Principle" is said to be how he organized his workload and priorities. He recognized that great time management means being effective as well as efficient. In other words, we must spend our time on things that are important and not just on those that are urgent. To do this, and to minimize the stress of having too many tight deadlines, we need to understand this distinction:

- Important activities have an outcome that leads to us achieving our goals, whether professional or personal.
- Urgent activities demand immediate attention and are usually associated with achieving someone else's goals. They are often the ones we concentrate on.

When we know which activities are important and which are urgent, we can over-come the natural tendency to focus on unimportant urgent activities, so that we can clear enough time to do what's essential for our success. This is the way we move from "firefighting" into a position where we can grow our businesses and our careers.

List all your tasks and activities and put them into one of the following categories:

- Important and urgent; unforeseen or left aside until the last minute: always plan some free time during the day
- Important but not urgent: take enough time
- Not important but urgent: reschedule or delegate
- Not important and not urgent: ignore and cancel

Conclusion? Important tasks are often much more useful than urgent ones, so make the important tasks your priority.

PARKINSON'S LAW
The idea behind the Eisenhower model is Parkinson's Law, which says that work tends to expand to fill the time available for the work's completion. It was formulated

in 1958 by Cyril Parkinson, who noticed that the number of people employed in a bureaucracy grows by 5–7% a year irrespective of the amount of work there is to be done. He cited two reasons for this: managers want to manage larger departments than their immediate peers, and managers create work to amplify their importance. We see the same effect more generally. If someone is hired to do a particular task, he or she will tend to expand that task. So what lesson can we draw from this? Demand for things automatically adjusts to coincide with the availability of those things. Although this can certainly be motivating for individuals, it is not always useful for organizations. Possibly it also explains why "busy" has become one of the most frequently heard words in today's communication departments. When a coworker asks how you are, what's the usual response? Exactly: "Busy, busy, busy!" Now, why is that?

Another determining factor when it comes to prioritizing is which competences you already have or can quickly bring on board. If the department is unable to cope with a task because it has neither the necessary competences nor the budget to acquire them, then you will have to step on the brakes. Or perhaps the issue is merely urgent, and therefore not important enough?

Parkinson was a man of many laws. His Law of Triviality states that the time spent on any item on an agenda is in inverse proportion to the money involved. Parkinson's thinking on incompetence in companies was elaborated by Laurence Peter and Raymond Hull (1969) to give us the Peter Principle, which states that in a hierarchy every employee tends to rise to his level of incompetence.

You can prioritize until you're blue in the face, but if you are subsequently unable to say no, time management will continue to be a problem. And let's be honest: saying no is not the most honed skill among communication professionals. Yet saying no could be a whole lot easier if your team agrees on a clear set of priorities together.

10 DO'S AND DON'TS

1   Don't treat strategic choices as if they are set in stone. They're not.
    You can go back and change those choices if you have good cause to do so.

2   Do be critical. Refer to the choices you made in the other building blocks;
    are they truly the best possible choices? And are they innovative enough?

3   Do develop your game plan together. Just as in the other building blocks,
    you have to proactively work together to arrive at clear shared choices.

4   Do beware of armchair experts: those people—there can be lots of them—who
    are eager to "pitch in" to the strategy. Ask yourselves who you really need in
    order to formulate a sound operational strategy and set the right priorities.

5   Do make sure that you can explain how the choices in your game plan are
    linked to your vision, ambitions, and KPIs.

6   Don't allow your plans to devolve into a long checklist of activities.
    Besides not showing anything, lists also lead to endless, pointless discussion.

7   Do distinguish between what is urgent and what is important when devising
    your game plan. The Communication Strategy Framework is solely about what
    is important.

8   Do make strategic choices comprehensible by using inspiring and clear
    language and singling out flagship projects.

9   Don't make your operational strategy too generic. The choices you make
    have to be directly aligned to and effectuate your other choices, so be as
    specific as possible.

10 Do keep one another on track and speak up when necessary: to achieve
    impact, the department, the team, and each person individually has to strike
    the right balance between what appears important and what truly is.

THE GAME PLAN BUILDING BLOCK IS ABOUT PUTTING THE FINISHING TOUCHES
ON YOUR STRATEGY. WHAT ARE YOU ACTUALLY GOING TO DO? WHAT WILL YOU
DO FIRST, AND WHAT CAN WAIT UNTIL LATER? WHICH OPERATIONAL STRATEGIES
AND/OR FLAGSHIP PROJECTS WILL YOU CHOOSE, WHICH ONES WILL YOU PRIORI-
TIZE, AND WHY? THESE ARE THE CENTRAL QUESTIONS OF THIS BUILDING BLOCK.

YOUR SUCCESSS
DEPENDS ON YOUR
UNDERSTANDING
OF THE DYNAMICS
OF THE ARENA

ROBERT L. HEATH ON COMMUNICATION STRATEGY

COMMUNICATION STRATEGY

THE TERM STRATEGY REQUIRES MEANS/ENDS THINKING. BY WHAT MEANS CAN AN INDIVIDUAL OR ORGANIZATION ACHIEVE FAVORABLE OUTCOMES?

A KEY TO BEING AN EFFECTIVE COMMUNICATOR IS TO REALIZE THAT BECAUSE IT IS CONTEXTUALLY RELEVANT, STRATEGY EXISTS IN ARENAS WHERE COUNTER STRATEGIES, STATEMENTS AND COUNTERSTATEMENTS, OCCUR DYNAMICALLY. THE METAPHOR OF AN ARCHERY MATCH IS APT, AND NECESSARILY EMPHASIZES HOW MULTIVOCAL STRATEGIC COMMUNICATION IS. ONE ARCHER CASTS (SHOOTS) THREE ARROWS. THAT IS LIKE UNIVOCAL COMMUNICATION, ONE MESSAGE AND EFFECT. BUT ONE ARCHER'S SCORE DOES NOT ACKNOWLEDGE OTHER ARCHERS' (OR VOICES) STRATEGIC SKILL.

STRATEGY PRESUMES AND ENCOUNTERS COUNTERSTRATEGY. INDIVIDUALS AND ORGANIZATIONS SEEK TO GET OTHERS TO AGREE WITH THEM IN ORDER TO GAIN REWARDS AND AVOID BAD OUTCOMES. HOW SUCCESSFUL THEY ARE DEPENDS ON THEIR UNDERSTANDING OF THE DYNAMICS OF THE ARENA AND THEIR ABILITY TO ADAPT SO AS TO COMMUNICATE IN WAYS THAT ARE EFFECTIVE, EFFICIENT, ETHICAL, AND ENGAGING.

Robert L. Heath, Ph.D.
Professor of public relations
University of Houston, United States of America

CASE: AN INTERNAL COMMUNICATION STRATEGY FOR COOLDAYS

Note:
This case is fictional ←

CoolDays is a leading soft drink manufacturer in Middle America. Its largest market is Mexico (40%), followed by the United States (25%) and Argentina (20%). The company has a permanent workforce of 1,900 employees. CoolDays produces three different kinds of soft drinks: CoolDays Red, CoolDays Blue (a light version of CoolDays Red made with aspartame), and CoolDays Green. CoolDays Green was launched in 2008 and its unique selling point in the soft drink market is that it's organic. CoolDays Green is immensely popular in the age group of 25- to 45-year-olds, particularly among graduates, who see the beverage as a sensible alternative to other less healthy soft drinks.

In recent years, CoolDays has been struggling. Sales of CoolDays Red and CoolDays Blue have been declining for the last nine years running and are under enormous pressure. Only CoolDays Green revenues are rising every year, and this is what is keeping CoolDays in the black.

Historically, the lion's share of the company's marketing budget has been spent on CoolDays Red and CoolDays Blue—the longtime key brands on which the company grew. However, even hefty marketing outlays, mainly on advertising, have not been able to reverse declining revenues. More marketing does not seem likely to help. Realizing that something had to be done, the management board hired Fernandez, Grillo & Fernandez, a renowned consultancy firm, to conduct an in-depth analysis and devise a growth strategy. The consultants conclude that the future of CoolDays Red and CoolDays Blue looks pretty bleak. The future of CoolDays Green, by constrast, looks exceptionally bright, because it taps into the growing demand for organic and healthy (or healthier) soft drinks.

AN INTERNAL COMMUNICATION STRATEGY FOR A COMPANY THAT NEEDS TO DRASTICALLY CHANGE COURSE TO STAY AFLOAT

A rigorous intervention is agreed, entailing a sizable reduction in investments in CoolDays Red and CoolDays Blue. In real terms, this will mean the closure of seven obsolete production locations and distribution centers over the next three years. CoolDays Green is manufactured at three extremely modern, efficient plants; operations there will continue. It is hoped that CoolDays Green production will expand in the future, but this remains uncertain for now. Moreover, the management board doesn't know yet at which locations that might be. Consequently, 30% of the company's employees have to be laid off in the next three years. At this stage it remains unclear exactly which jobs will be cut, but the affected production locations and distribution centers have already been chosen. A handful of employees at the headquarters in Mexico will lose their jobs too. Also, the marketing strategy is to be drastically overhauled. Most of the marketing budget is being earmarked to contribute to further growing CoolDays Green. Six months from now the company will launch one of the largest marketing campaigns in the history of CoolDays, focused completely on CoolDays Green. The ad agency will be briefed in a few days' time.

Although the CEO is very pleased with the new strategy, he realizes it will have a massive impact on staff. CoolDays is a family-run firm, and many of the employees have worked there their whole lives. Emotionally, he is struggling with this decision. What's more, the CEO is finding it difficult to explain the quite complex and specialized strategy in a way that his employees can grasp. Above all, he wants them to understand that this strategy is the only viable option. And he wants to avoid giving them any false hopes. On the one hand, he feels deep concern about what will happen to his employees and therefore has made careful internal communication a priority; on the other, the decision to lay off 30% of the company's workforce in the next three years and kill its familiar old brands is a fait accompli.

The Chief Communications Officer thinks the time is right to make some major strides in engagement. She calls her team together and they get to work with the Communication Strategy Framework. Go to page 132 to read about her choices and focus. Would you handle it the same way?

INTERNAL COMMUNICATION STRATEGY FOR

INTERNAL SITUATION

ORGANIZATION

- Unavoidable intervention: closure of 7 locations, layoff of 270 people over 3 years
- Limited communication about bleak prospects
- Hiring of consultancy firm has created anxiety

COMMUNICATION STYLE

- Employees love the company, talk about it in positive terms
- Style is open and honest and mostly top-down

VISION

RELEVANT TRENDS IN THE FIELD

Vision on communication

Internal = external

Most impact: management/employee conversations

Communication means have to support and facilitate conversations

Role of the department

Develop a comprehensible and appealing story

Develop auxiliary communication platforms

Strengthen managers' conversational capacity (tools)

AMBITION

CORE VALUES

1) Open, honest, careful communication
2) Hands-on support for managers
3) Focus on listening and two-way communication

CORE TASK

1) Fully inform employees so they understand the new course and its consequences
2) Minimize anxiety by providing thorough explanations and a listening ear
3) Further enhance engagement among employees who will stay on

EXTERNAL SITUATION

TRENDS

- Drastic changes in consumer preferences
- Frequent NGO obesity campaigns
- Responsible companies put on a pedestal; "bad" companies under fire

ISSUES AND MOOD

- CoolDays is a big favorite in political and media circles, but the obesity issue is making inroads there, too
- Frequent critical posts online about sugar and aspartame in connection with CoolDays
- Shrinking base of support in government

COOLDAYS' CHANGE PROGRAM

...DERS

...ard, strategy director, marketing director,
...... have to support the communication strategy
and ensure staff support the newly charted course

PARTNERS

Board of directors, HR department, and top and
middle management have to join forces to achieve the
communication strategy

Note! Formulate core messages here too

ACCOUNTABILITY

SUCCESS FACTORS

1) Commitment from top management and cooperation from middle
management; 2) Alignment of internal and external communication;
3) Employee satisfaction with communication

RESPONSIBILITY

1) Management is responsible for internal communication
2) CC department is responsible for practical support in the form
   of coaching, training, and means

KPIs

1) Managers feel they are getting the right communication support;
2) Employees feel informed and taken seriously and understand the
whys and wherefores; 3) Internal and external communication are
fully synchronized; 4) Messages are timely, straightforward, and
comprehensible; 5) Communication considers factory conditions
and communication limitations

MEASUREMENT

1) Focus group meetings between managers and staff; 2) Additional
questions in annual employee engagement survey; 3) Brief (online + print)
poll of employees (after 1 month)

GAME PLAN

OPERATIONAL STRATEGY

Foundation: Managers provide information
about the change strategy in stages using
texts and visuals **Emphasis:** Personal communication by and with managers **Means:**
Existing channels (memos, intranet, staff
magazine) PLUS personal communication
PLUS practical support by managers (tools,
training, etc.)

PRIORITIES

1) Message and communication training
   for managers, plus tools (Q&A, PPT, etc.)
2) Launch of newly charted course (on
   date X) at staff meetings at all locations
3) Personal letters and memos to employees

Note! On the same day as external communication launch

RESOURCES

PEOPLE

- Dedicated task force (comms director and comms advisor,
  social media expert, spokesperson, HR director, marketing
  manager, divisions manager, external advisor
- Agency to be engaged to develop concept and means

BUDGET

Budget estimate: 250 k. Agency costs = 150 k.
Communication means and channels = 50 k.
Miscellaneous = 50 k

THE COMMUNICATION STRATEGY FRAMEWORK

How to make the Framework work for you

GETTING
TO WORK

WHERE DO WE GO FROM HERE?

Great! The Framework is going to help people develop the right strategy. But how do you ensure it actually works?

At the very least you need to have a good grasp of the field and trends and how they'll impact your practice. That's step one.

Absolutely, I agree. That's a key question—one that doesn't get the attention it deserves.

Exactly. But obviously there's no simple answer.

There are theories and gurus galore, but they often have widely different views.

True, what it all hinges on in this profession is realizing what the consequences of a specific communication method could be.

But what else do you need? How do you guarantee an effective strategy?

In my own consultancy practice I see that the demands on communication professionals are continually increasing. And they themselves are raising the bar too—and rightly so. After all, the stakes can be high.

Betteke

Frank

THIS BOOK WASN'T JUST CHURNED OUT ON A COMPUTER BUT IS THE RESULT OF INTENSIVE DIALOGUE—SOMETIMES FACE-TO-FACE, MORE OFTEN BY EMAIL AND WHATSAPP—THAT LED TO ALL KINDS OF FASCINATING DISCUSSIONS. STRATEGY DEVELOPMENT IS AN INTERACTIVE PROCESS, AND SO WAS THE WRITING OF THIS BOOK.

You talk a lot about business focus. I think that's an interesting concept, but could you explain it a little more?

Sure. Basically, it's about wanting to know what the organization's ambitions are and having the drive to help achieve them. But that takes sensitivity, analytical ability, social skills, and a can-do attitude. And of course a good balance in the team.

A balance of what exactly?

Between strategy, coordination, and execution. That's essential, don't you think?

Sure. Also, it's vital that as a professional or a department you formulate a clear profile—that you know how you want others to see you.

Also, to think about your role and positioning and get it across clearly within the organization.

Is that leadership, in a sense?

Yes, I think so. The fact is, if you want to play at the highest level, you have to show leadership. You have to know what you stand for and what you want and be assertive about it.

Leadership in communication—that's becoming increasingly important. But what does it actually mean?

Always being a step ahead of everyone else in everything that's communication-related. Showing that you're the expert and a serious discussion partner.

But beyond that, what does it take to achieve real impact?

New insights. An element of surprise. Making bold moves. Certainly not staying on the same well-worn path. You have to go off the beaten track, be adventurous.

Be bold. I like that, and it's important. That's something we can't stress enough. Making choices is scary. But that's OK. Playing it safe is often the easiest option, but not necessarily the best.

Making choices can also be unsettling because it means you reject some options; those roads are no longer open to you. You're betting all your chips on one thing. But that's what strategy is all about. Making choices.

FOUR
MYTHS
DEBUNKED

MYTH:
WITHOUT A SEAT ON THE EXECUTIVE TEAM,
OUR DEPARTMENT WILL NEVER MAKE AN IMPACT

Do you need to be a member of the management team to be able to make a real difference? It stands to reason that a communication department is stronger if it has strong ties with the board. A short chain of command and C-suite support will certainly enhance the impact of communication. These days, most communication directors report directly to the CEO or another management board member.

At three-quarters of European organizations the communication function is invited to strategic decision-making meetings (see www.europeancommunicationmonitor. eu). That leaves one-quarter at which they are not. The question is, is that a problem? Should the communication profession even want to be a part of discussions about organizational strategy or other "big" topics? Or is it enough to exert an influence by other means? We believe that the added value of communication professionals lies in their capacity to help executives make better decisions. Membership of the management team is by no means a must; being a part of the dominant coalition of people who matter in the organization and influence decisions formally and informally—that is.

Having impact primarily means you ensure the organization makes better decisions.

EVERY FIELD HAS ITS MYTHS, AND COMMUNICATION IS NO EXCEPTION. THESE MYTHS CAN LEAD THE ORGANIZATION ASTRAY AND STUNT THE DEVELOPMENT OF ITS COMMUNICATION FUNCTION. WE DEBUNK THE FOUR MOST COMMON ONES.

MYTH:
WE COULD BE MUCH MORE EFFECTIVE IF WE DIDN'T HAVE TO WORRY ABOUT EXECUTION

With the advance of large-scale industry in the mid-1800s, companies found themselves facing three challenges: how to produce more at lower cost, how to combat "laziness" among workers, and how to structure work processes to maximize the potential of machines and human resources. The solution to these problems came from Frederic Taylor, who in around 1900 introduced the principle of scientific management. To clear up the gray area of what could be expected from employees, he came up with a division between thinking and doing. Thinking was the responsibility of managers, doing of workers.

Productivity shot up. Enjoyment in working did not. Pretty quickly, that sparked the idea that managers should oversee not only the tasks to be performed but also the personal wellbeing of workers (human relations). However, execution remained firmly distinct from leading and advising.

Modern management theories take a very different view, particularly in the knowledge-based and creative professions. The separation between thinking and doing is obsolete. As Donald Schön (1983) observed, a reflective practitioner is constantly thinking about the actions they take, and it is in this thoughtful action that their strength lies. Thus, thinking and acting ought to go hand in hand. We are all for this kind of "thacting." Like we said before, nothing is more strategic than crafting the right opening sentence. Furthermore, if you as a department have not mastered the basics—the doing—then chances are slim that anyone will welcome your input on those matters.

Thinking and doing/acting must go together.

MYTH:
COMMUNICATION BELONGS TO THE COMMUNICATION DEPARTMENT

Lots of communication professionals view themselves (or their team) as the organization's key communicator. You hardly need us to tell you that's nonsense. Everyone in an organization communicates. And that is nothing new; organizing anything at all necessitates communication. However, in this digital day and age of changing ideas about the roles of managers and staff, more and more people who are not communication professionals are creating publicity, and sometimes even making the news. That has led to questions about what communication departments are actually in charge of.

The consensus is that their principal function is to help others in the organization communicate better. By laying out the rules of the game and providing support using the right means, by coaching, training, orchestrating, holding a mirror up to the organization, and by reflecting with one another. That does not mean the department no longer implements communication. On the contrary, its aim should be not that the department itself communicates and connects well but that others in the organization communicate well and maintain their connections. It might seem like semantics, but this slight shift in how you think about the profession makes a world of difference.

Good communication is the responsibility of everyone in the organization.

MYTH:
THE BIGGER THE DEPARTMENT,
THE GREATER THE IMPACT

The size of a department is no indicator of its impact. We have seen departments that staff dozens but never actually consider what they are doing or to what purpose, and we've seen teams of just three or four expert professionals who manage to move mountains. Much more significant than size is how the department views its own role and added value (and how that is put into practice), and the mindset of the people in the department.

This vision on your role and added value articulate how you aim to make the difference. By extension, it makes clear what the organization would lack without the communication department. The size of the department has no effect on this vision, but only on what you choose to do and not do, and how you do what you do. These days, departmental structures are increasingly flexible. Those with a small core staff and network of specialized independent contractors are swiftly changing from an exception to the rule. Of course, not everyone has what it takes to be a top in-company professional or external specialist advisor; that requires very specific and very exceptional competences.

Impact is determined by the choices you make.

AUTHENTIC COMMUNICATION
WARRANTS CAUTIOUS STRATEGIC STRATEGY AND PLANNING

RONÉL RENSBURG ON COMMUNICATION STRATEGY

COMMUNICATION STRATEGY

DURING THE PAST DECADE COMMUNICATION SCHOLARS HAVE BEEN UNSWERVINGLY ADVOCATING STRATEGIC COMMUNICATION MANAGEMENT.

THE RESURGENCE OF CULTURAL, SOCIAL AND POLITICAL CONFLICT AND CORPORATE PRESSURES ACROSS THE WORLD, ALSO COMPELLED COMMUNI-CATION PRACTITIONERS TO MORE CAREFULLY EXPLORE, PLAN, IMPLEMENT AND EVALUATE THE COMMUNICATION ENDEAVORS FOR WHICH THEY ARE ACCOUNTABLE. THE ONSET OF FAKE NEWS AND FETTERED COMMUNICATI-ON CONTENT CAN BREAK COUNTRY, CORPORATE AND INDIVIDUAL REPU-TATIONS, ACCENTUATING THAT THERE IS A GROWING VALUE IN SEEKING AUTHENTIC COMMUNICATION. AUTHENTIC COMMUNICATION WARRANTS CAUTIOUS STRATEGIC STRATEGY AND PLANNING.

THE TIME IS RIFE —NOW MORE THAN EVER— FOR THE PROVISION OF AN ACADEMICALLY SECURE AND CONSTRUCTIVE PRACTICAL COMMUNICATION FRAMEWORK DURING STRATEGIC JUDGMENT.

Ronél Rensburg, Ph.D.
Full Professor of Communication Management
University of Pretoria
Founding member of the Centre for Communication and Reputation Management, South Africa

HIGH REQUIREMENTS, RISING EXPECTATIONS

Communication is getting plenty of attention in boardrooms these days. It has come into its own as a full-fledged management instrument and communication managers have gained a place at the top of the ladder in quite a few organizations. According to the European Communication Monitor, the advisory influence of communication professionals is on the rise in Europe, at least among respondents. This means that what they say is taken seriously by top management.

MEANINGFUL ROLE
Can we as professionals lean back and rest on our proverbial laurels? Not a chance. One-third of communication directors polled by the Monitor are still not a trusted advisor, and more than 20% of all communication professionals have no advisory influence at all. Consequently, they have to push hard to be heard. And that is very odd. After all, not only does communication play a vital role in the success of organizations, but serious sums are invested in it, too.

THE GROWING NEED TO ADD VALUE
After the fallout of the economic crisis, which left many communication departments a fraction of their former size, now we are seeing investments in communication inch back up. Though the crisis left deep scars, awareness of the importance of excellent communication has, if anything, grown stronger. This is attested by data from the European Communication Monitor (www. europeancommunicationmonitor.eu), led by professors from renowned universities within the framework of the European Public Relations Education and Research Association (EUPRERA) together with the European Associa-

INCREASINGLY, ORGANIZATIONS ARE DEMANDING THAT THEIR COMMUNICATION DEPARTMENTS MAKE DEMONSTRABLE CONTRIBUTIONS TOWARD THE REALIZATION OF OBJECTIVES. THEY WANT THEIR COMMUNICATION DEPARTMENTS TO BE BUSINESS-FOCUSED. AND THE DEPARTMENTS WANT THAT TOO. BUT HOW DO YOU DO THAT?

tion of Communication Directors (EACD). In the 2017 edition of the Monitor, the majority of respondents stated that communication became only more instrumental to their organization's success over the prior year. That also means communication departments are being expected to deliver more. Our own interviews with senior executives and other inhouse customers likewise reveal a real awareness of the importance of professional communication. In fact, expectations are extremely high, especially in boardrooms, which expect their communication departments to continually add more value and want to know what communication and the communication department are contributing to the organization's strategic ambitions and priorities. However, we've also found that conceptions differ in practice as to the measure of added value communication can deliver. Where some departments point to positive press coverage, others talk about bolstering employee engagement or building a strong reputation.

AT WHAT LEVEL IS YOUR COMMUNICATION DEPARTMENT OPERATING?
In our long practice in academia (Betteke) and consultancy (Frank), we have done extensive work on optimizing the communication function in organizations, more specifically, on how to design and structure it for maximum efficiency and efficacy. In the course of that work, we have talked to many communication professionals, of course, but also with senior executives, other inhouse customers, and opinion leaders in the field. One thing that has become apparent to us is that most communication departments are on the right track, but not all are where they need and want to be. This is not surprising, given that the desire for communication to play a more strategic role is still fairly recent; who could blame the professional for struggling with this new set of expectations?

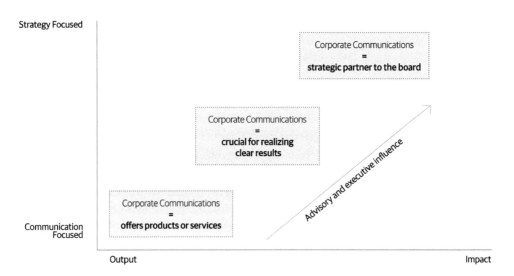

Figure 9. Impact Model (Körver, 2012)

Körver's Impact Model is a tool that can be used to gauge the level at which a communication department is operating. Experience shows that a department can only advance to a higher level after it has fully mastered the previous level. Many departments operate at level 1, some at a cautious level 2. The main problem is that many are still approaching things

IN PRACTICE, PLAYING THE BOARDROOM GAME WELL CAN BE QUITE A CHALLENGE

from the narrow angle of communication means, with too much emphasis on output and too little on the desired impact. Our meetings with communication directors at transnational companies and opinion leaders from across the globe affirmed this view, but also demonstrate that practitioners do aspire to perform at a higher level. Yet this is more easily said than done. In practice, playing the boardroom game well can be quite a challenge.

TIES WITH TOP MANAGEMENT

A short chain of command to the board and management puts the communication department in a stronger position, and if board members genuinely recognize communication's value to the organization's business and strategy, the communication department may even be able to participate at the highest level. Of course, the communication director (or whatever the title used) also has a hand in this. He or she has to have an extensive network, access to strategic and other information, and to understand how their work ties in with the organizational strategy. Also essential is that the communication director can show how communication impacts the organization's success. Lastly, he or she has to invest in forging relationships with the CEO and other key players in the organization. The better their chemistry, the better the chance this person will be accepted as a trusted advisor.

BUSINESS-FOCUSED COMMUNICATION

COMMUNICATION ENABLES BETTER DECISION-MAKING

Many communication departments take a tactical, near-term approach to communication. But this fails to capitalize on communication's real, full potential. A strong communication department understands and responds to top management's priorities and draws on its knowledge of concerns in society and what matters to staff, customers, and stakeholders to accelerate and improve the decision-making process at the top.

THE COMMUNICATION FUNCTION BALANCES STRATEGY, COORDINATION, AND EXECUTION

Traditionally, communication departments are strongest at the operational level, in the execution. But what they should really be concerned with is strategy and coordination; this is where the real opportunities are for business-focused

LEVEL 1
STRATEGY & CONCEPT
Developing strategies and concepts that help realize on organization's strategic objectives

LEVEL 2
COORDINATION & CONNECTION
Coordinating and steering communication processes and connecting communication strategy and operational strategy by facilitating, counceling, and tooling

LEVEL 3
EXECUTION
Implementing programs and developing means aligned with the communication strategy

Figure 10. Communication Activities Pyramid

BUSINESS-FOCUSED COMMUNICATION HAS A MAJOR INFLUENCE ON HOW COM-
MUNICATION AND ITS VARIOUS FUNCTIONS ARE ORGANIZED. IT AFFECTS THE WAY
IN WHICH COMMUNICATION DEPARTMENTS ARE STRUCTURED AND WHAT GETS
PRIORITIZED. BUT WHAT DOES BUSINESS-FOCUSED COMMUNICATION ACTUALLY
ENTAIL?

communication. It's only logical that communication directors are particularly interested in boosting their departments' strategic knowledge and knowhow. A senior
advisor who also has a good command of strategy can more deftly switch gears
between business and communication and even talk on a level with line managers.

COMMUNICATION OBJECTIVES ARE LINKED TO ORGANIZATIONAL OBJECTIVES
AND STRATEGIC PRIORITIES
Many communication plans lack a clear translation of the strategic objectives
and priorities into goals for communication. Business-focused communication
presupposes that all internal and external communication is premised on the
organizational strategy. This is the only way to ensure a firm focus on the proverbial 20% of the activities that achieve 80% of the results. Linking communication
objectives and programs to specific organizational objectives and priorities makes
the communication department much more relevant to line management.

RESEARCH, ANALYSIS, AND RENEWAL PLAY AN INSTRUMENTAL ROLE
To help senior executives in make better decisions, communication profressionals
need to employ research and analysis. Ideally, research on things such as
reputation, media publicity, stakeholders, and target audiences is carried out
on a planned, ongoing basis. The communication department can also provide
targeted actionable feedback on the performance of the organization and its
members. This kind of research and analysis can fuel renewal and thus serve as a
touchstone (Are we on the right track?) and a compass (What is the right track?)
both in the communication department and outside it.

COMMUNICATION RESULTS ARE CLEAR
Which communication objectives have been achieved, and which ones have not?
To which organizational objectives did the department make a demonstrable
contribution? What went well? What could have gone better? Making clear what
the impact of the chosen communication strategy is and how it contributes to
achieving the organization's strategic objectives is extremely valuable. Not only

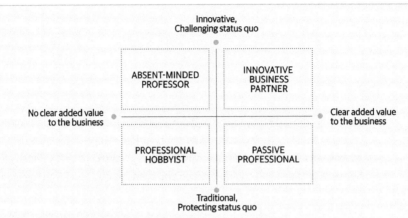

Figure 11. Typology of communication departments (Körver, 2012)

The absent-minded professor

This department is innovative, but it's not clear what it is contributing to the business goals. Innovations are insufficiently aligned to the needs of internal customers. The department seems to be wrapped up in itself and uses a lot of jargon; its core focus and only concern is communication. Statements you are likely to hear: "They don't understand us" or "They speak a different language." The department is very innovative and questions the status quo, but tends to choose the wrong areas to focus on. Its added value is minimal.

The professional hobbyist

This department does not make any definable contributions to the business goals and is insufficiently innovative. Statements you are likely to hear: "This is how we've always done things" and "That wouldn't work here." Though its intentions are good, it tends to operate on autopilot, without any real driving forces for innovation. The department functions like an island and is hardly involved in broader processes. Its added value is low.

The innovative business partner

This department both makes definable contributions to achieving the business goals and is innovative. It has satisfied internal customers and has a convincing story about what it has to offer the organization. The only danger with this department is that it might get too far ahead of the game, but its business focus and subsequent strong relationships with internal customers can prevent that. This department is an innovative business partner that delivers real added value.

The passive professional

This department does contribute to the business goals, but its stance is conservative and passive. Statement you are likely to hear: "We're treated like an afterthought." That's hardly surprising. Although internal customers do recognize the department's added value, they perceive it to be marginal. In their eyes, the department is stuck in outmoded approaches, is not innovative and proactive enough, and is unwilling to come up with new ideas.

can the resulting insights be used to set or adjust communication policy and budgets, they also contribute to "good governance," enabling the department to legitimate its activities to its staff and the rest of the organization from time to time.

TOP MANAGEMENT IS ACTIVELY INVOLVED IN COMMUNICATION
Though myriad studies have established the value of CEO involvement in communication, it is still far from standard in practice. Having formal structures that foster collaboration and mutual understanding can help. Some companies create reputation or brand boards in which the CEO plays an active role. Appointing a communication manager with a background in business administration or line management can open doors too, but if they don't know much about communication it can also create a whole new set of problems. For communication professionals, it is certainly a wise idea to learn more about business administration and policy processes.

COMMUNICATION PROFESSIONALS SPEAK THE LANGUAGE OF THE BUSINESS
Many communication professionals are passionate about their profession, but lack the skills to exercise a broader strategic role, especially in areas like financial management, strategy development, and organizational development and change. Yet without that knowledge, communication runs the risk of being dismissed as ancillary to the organization's success. Communication professionals, therefore, have to make it their business to know what is happening in the organization, and to steer clear of communication jargon as much as possible.

PROFESSIONAL HOBBYIST OR INNOVATIVE BUSINESS PARTNER?
A typology of communication departments developed by Frank Körver (2012) characterizes four types of departments that are common in real-world practice, from very conservative to continuously innovating, and from not focused to highly focused on contributing to the organizational objectives. To risk stating the obvious, focusing on organizational objectives is not the same thing as kowtowing to the boss. That's just servility. Being a true business partner is about offering a professional service; about serving the business from a foundation of personal professional standards, always while staying loyal toward the other, critical toward yourself.

THERE IS
NO PLANNING
WITHOUT STRATEGY
AND A LONG-RANGE
PERSPECTIVE

MARIA APARECIDA FERRARI ON COMMUNICATION STRATEGY

COMMUNICATION STRATEGY

IN AN EVER MORE COMPLEX AND CONNECTED WORLD, COMMUNICATIONS PROFESSIONALS MUST PLAN COMMUNICATION STRATEGIES THAT FACILITATE AN EFFECTIVE AND EFFICIENT ACHIEVEMENT OF OBJECTIVES.

THERE IS NO PLANNING WITHOUT STRATEGY AND A LONG-RANGE PERSPECTIVE. IT IS FOR THIS REASON THAT STRATEGY IS THE PREFERRED MEANS FOR ACHIEVING ESTABLISHED OBJECTIVES.

TWO ELEMENTS ARE OF EXTREME IMPORTANCE IN THE DEFINITION OF A COMMUNICATION STRATEGY, NAMELY SCENARIO ANALYSIS AND THE IDENTIFICATION OF THE STAKEHOLDERS.

IN THE FINAL ANALYSIS, A WELL-DEFINED STRATEGY WILL DRIVE COHERENT, COHESIVE AND CONTINUAL COMMUNICATION THAT WILL FACILITATE THE LEGITIMACY OF THE ORGANIZATION WITH ITS PUBLICS.

Maria Aparecida Ferrari, Ph.D.
Professor of public relations
Universidade de São Paulo, Brasil

LEADERSHIP
IN COMMUNICATION

Whereas management is mainly a technical process of taking charge, leadership centers on the personal capacity to inspire others and influence people to do things differently. Leadership tends to be defined as a process through which an individual influences a group of individuals to accomplish a specific goal. "To manage for tomorrow takes a visionary leader capable of assessing the present and seeing the potential that lies in the future," writes John A. Koten (2004, p. xx) in *Building Trust*. In other words, leaders look ahead and see opportunities.

PROMOTING YOURSELF

Real leadership takes more than just the ability to look ahead and see opportunities. You also need to position yourself as a leader by creating your own platform and promoting yourself. This is not something that comes easily to everyone. It takes a specific kind of personality, and it is what separates leaders from specialists. The specialist performs a job and excels at it; the leader probes why things are done the way they are and comes up with novel alternatives. A leader is capable of changing how others look at things and of inspiring them to do things differently. A leader's success hinges on the support of followers. In other words, other people determine whether you show leadership.

We do wonder, however, whether the concepts of management and leadership might not just be flip sides of the same coin: both refer to a kind of leadership style adopted by the manager.

TRUSTED ADVISOR

A communication professional who wants to be taken seriously by top management and be a trusted advisor has to show leadership. The book *The Trusted*

MOST LEADERSHIP THEORIES DEFINE LEADERSHIP IN OPPOSITION TO MANAGEMENT. MANAGERS KEEP AN EYE ON THE BUSINESS; LEADERS ELEVATE THE BUSINESS TO NEW HEIGHTS.

Advisor by David Maister, Charles Green, and Robert Galford (2002) is widely read in the business consultancy world, but the insights it offers are equally valid for communication professionals seeking to enlarge their role in the organization, certainly now that the "age of hyperspecialization" is waning and organizations are looking for strategically savvy generalists.

According to Maister and his co-authors, a trusted advisor is simultaneously an expert in building, maintaining, and sustaining relationships with clients and in supplying practical, substantiated, and professional advice that has real added value for their client. The effect of your advice is a product of the quality of your advice multiplied by its acceptance.

To be a trusted advisor, say Maister et al. (p. 1), you need three basic skills ("the territory of the trusted advisor"):

Competence 1: Earning trust. You have to prove that you genuinely want to help your client and that you're in it for the long haul instead of just trying to maximize the short-term benefit to you. To do that, you need to invest in the relationship and show that you will do what you say you will do. You have to be willing to "give" and show some form of caring.

Competence 2: Giving advice effectively. Giving advice is more than an objective, rational application of practical knowledge. A good advisor also considers the personal, emotional dimension of their advisory role and quickly understands each individual client's preferred style of interaction. This enables the advisor to deal with the client in the manner that the client finds most comfortable.

Competence 3: Building relationships. According to Maister, a relationship based on equality has the greatest effect. Your client has to trust you as an advisor, but also as a person. To a large extent, being a good advisor comes down to cultivating a bond of trust with a client. Listening, being truly interested in the person and showing appreciation is key. Your objective is not to score engagements but to build relationships.

Maister et al. (pp. 85–89) set out five steps for achieving trust-based relationships:

Engage: Make sure you are worthy of being spoken to in an open, truthful manner about the issue at hand. What issues is your client truly concerned about? It is about connecting your expertise to problems that affect the client.

Listen: Listen actively and empathetically to what is said and what is unspoken. And do not only listen, you must also do something to give the client the experience of having been listened to so that the client comes to believe you understand him or her.

Frame: Crystallize and clarify the complexity of the client's problem. Rather than immediately thinking about solutions, fully analyze the problem and define what it is first. This may involve redefining the client's issues in a political or emotional framework.

Envision: Concretize a specific vision (and choice) among possible future states so that the client begins to understand his or her true goals. Together with the client you envision how the end result might look, without prematurely giving in to the temptation to solve the problem.

Commit: Ensure that the client understands what it will take to achieve the vision, and to help the client find the determination to do what is necessary. This step is all about managing and establishing mutual expectations and actions.

Maister's books may be written for external consultants, but his insights are equally valid for advisors working inhouse. They, too, need to be trusted advisors to be effective. "A thought leader is an individual or firm that prospects, clients, referral sources, intermediaries and even competitors recognize as one of the foremost authorities in selected areas of specialization, resulting in its being the go-to individual or organization for said expertise," say Russ Alan Prince and Bruce Rogers (2012). This describes precisely what we envision a communication department should be: a thought leader on communication and communication management.

PLAYING AT THE HIGHEST LEVEL

Five tips for communication professionals who want to play at the highest level:

1   Build up a strong network in the organization— one that extends beyond the communication function, ensuring that others know to come to you when needed.
2   Gain access to information. Keep abreast of what is happening within and outside the organization. Don't let yourself be caught by surprise.
3   Understand how your work ties in with the organizational strategy. You need to have a clear picture of how your communication department intends to deliver added value.
4   Make your impact on the success of the enterprise clear and share this insight with the top level of the organization.
5   Invest in your relationship with the CEO. The chemistry between you will in large part determine your acceptance as a trusted advisor.

BE PART OF THE DOMINANT COALITION

If the communication department is to operate at a real strategic level, it has to be part of the dominant coalition. This is the group of people who form the locus of power and influence how things are done in the organization. The dominant coalition does not necessarily mirror the organizational hierarchy; rather, it is the informal group of people who matter, whose opinions are consulted, and whose clear-sightedness and added value have earned the trust of others in the organization.

If you want to be a part of the dominant coalition, you must not show hesitation, fail to make choices, be ignorant of who's doing what in the organization, do whatever you please, focus solely on output, try to be a Jack-of-all-trades, not fail to do the groundwork.

If you do aim to be a part of the dominant coalition, you must demonstrate vision and strategic muscle, have solid relationships, know the members of the board and management and understand their priorities, be able to point to your own impact, carve out a strong position for the department, work hard, and always offer fresh angles that no one else has thought of.

TEN
GOLDEN
RULES

THE COMMUNICATION STRATEGY FRAMEWORK

in action

MAKE THE COMMUNICATION STRATEGY FRAMEWORK WORK FOR YOU

TEN RULES THAT WILL HELP YOU TO APPLY THE COMMUNICATION STRATEGY
FRAMEWORK SUCCESSFULLY

1   Start with your vision on what communication contributes to the
    organization. This determines to a large extent where you will direct your ener-
    gy and your perspective on issues in and around the organization. Start with
    your vision, discuss what excellent communication means at your organization,
    and then what it means for you to excel as a communication professional. Think
    about what role you as a department, unit, or individual aim to play in or for the
    organization. Be specific, articulate it in a way that will appeal to others, capture
    it in a memorable catchphrase, and make this the touchstone for all your subse-
    quent choices.

2   Take an inclusive approach. Strategies are not and quite simply cannot be de-
    vised in isolation. Think carefully about who you will involve in the process, from
    your immediate coworkers to colleagues in other departments. We are strong
    believers in the power of diversity. If your strategy is about reputation, why not
    invite business or investor relations to contribute? Or, if it's about changes in the
    organization, get input from HR professionals. If it's about the development of a
    new social intranet, get the IT staff on board. Your strategy will only benefit.

3   Have fun with it. The quality of the process largely determines the end result, so make your strategy development a fun process. Instead of brainstorming sessions in a fluorescent-lit basement, gather in an open and airy room. Check any resentments at the door. Use inspiring working methods and create space for bold visions, but also keep your feet planted firmly on the ground. Be proud of what you create together. Make sure there's plenty of good coffee and tasty nibbles. And celebrate the end results together.

4   Take your time. Strategy development is neither a sleight of hand nor a list that can be checked off. It takes focus and critical and creative thinking. Make sure you have plenty of time for in-depth discussions. Nothing will kill creativity faster than a ticking clock. Not satisfied with the results of a work session? Then by all means schedule another and make firm agreements about what you plan to achieve. Discipline is crucial too. Don't arrive late to work sessions and never leave early to attend that other important meeting. The worst thing you can do is treat the process as though it's not important.

5. Prefer dialogue over debate. The strategy development process will raise a whole spectrum of subjects, some more sensitive than others. Tempers may flare, so be prepared. A healthy debate can be useful, but we prefer a meaningful dialogue. Listen to one another and understand each other. The objective is not to score points but to reach consensus. Then, and only then, will the strategy belong to everyone.

6. Make choices. The Communication Strategy Framework is designed to help you make choices. And making choices is essential, particularly in cases where resources are limited. In this book we've said that it is always better to be just a little uncertain about your strategy. "If you are entirely comfortable with your strategy, there's a strong chance it isn't very good. You need to be uncomfortable and apprehensive: true strategy is about placing bets and making hard choices" (Martin, 2014).

7. Diverge and converge. Before you delve into the details, explore your horizons. Consider options, describe scenarios, discuss the wide array of possibilities, and don't, whatever you do, dive down too fast. Make sure to stock up on flip charts and brown paper. Your aim is to discover links, narrow down options, and agree on what's essential. Make a clear distinction between must-haves and nice-to-haves by keeping your objective in mind and asking yourselves: What is this strategy for? Tip: read The Pyramid Principle by Barbara Minto (2008).

8. Concentrate on the things you can influence. All too often, work sessions devolve into arguments about things that we as communication professionals have no influence over. Whatever your feelings about the company's strategy, once that course has been set, you are stuck with it. Social media are here to stay, whether you like how they impact society or not. And cuts are usually irrevocable, so you had better accept it. Concentrate instead on the things that fall within your sphere of influence and responsibility. Complaining about matters you have no control over is simply a waste of time. So, don't.

9. Kill your darlings. We can't say it often enough: strategy means making choices. That may mean you have to cross off some options. Or that management is less than enthusiastic about your brilliant idea. So be it. Sometimes you have to kill your darlings. Getting rid of unnecessary baggage and anything that will never get internal support will only make your strategy that much better.

10. Get high-level backing. Having the support of your client, or the CEO, or the program director, puts you in a much stronger position and ensures your strategy will be taken more seriously. Engage your clients and other higher levels in the process. And be crystal clear about how your approach and the outcome (the strategy) will contribute to achieving the organization's objectives. It is up to you to be the storyteller of your strategy!

LAST BUT CERTAINLY NOT LEAST, REMEMBER THAT THE COMMUNICATION STRATEGY FRAMEWORK IS NEVER A STATIC MODEL. YOU CAN ALWAYS —AND SHOULD— ADAPT THE CONTENT OF THE PRESCRIBED EIGHT BUILDING BLOCKS TO FIT YOUR SPECIFIC (CHANGED) CONTEXT. CHANGE IT, REARRANGE IT, AND LET IT WORK FOR YOU!

PLANNING, RESEARCH AND MEASUREMENT ARE FUNDAMENTAL TO EVERY PIECE OF WORK

STEPHEN WADDINGTON **ON COMMUNICATION STRATEGY**

COMMUNICATION STRATEGY

A FORMAL PLANNING PROCESS WILL BRING RIGOUR AND DISCIPLINE TO YOUR WORK. IT'S A GOOD COMPANION TO CREATIVITY. YOU SHOULD BE ABLE TO SUMMARIZE A STRATEGIC COMMUNICATION PLAN ON A SINGLE PIECE OF PAPER AND BE ABLE TO EXPLAIN IT IN FIVE MINUTES. THIS DOESN'T MEAN DUMBING DOWN THE PLANNING PROCESS, BUT IS GOOD MANAGEMENT PRACTICE.

TAKING A 12 MONTH, OR EVEN QUARTERLY, OUTLOOK IS CHALLENGING WHEN OPERATING IN A PERIOD OF SEEMINGLY UNPRECEDENTED ECONOMIC AND POLITICAL UNCERTAINTY BUT ORGANISATIONS NEED TO CONTINUE TO MANAGE INVESTMENT AND TALENT. MY RECOMMENDATION IS TO TAKE THE LONGEST TERM OUTLOOK FEASIBLE FOR YOUR ORGANISATION BUT TEST, MEASURE AND ADAPT YOUR PLAN OVER TIME. REAL TIME MEASUREMENT AND AGILITY IS A REALITY FOR ANY MODERN PUBLIC RELATIONS TEAM

THERE CAN BE NO SHORTCUTS. PLANNING, RESEARCH AND MEASUREMENT ARE FUNDAMENTAL TO EVERY PIECE OF WORK. THEY'RE AS CRITICAL AS CREATIVE, CHANNELS AND EXECUTION.

Stephen Waddington
Partner and Chief Engagement Officer, Ketchum
Visiting Professor, Newcastle University, United Kingdom

BIBLIOGRAPHY

Adair, John (2009). *Effective Leadership: How to be a Successful Leader*. London, England: Pan Macmillan.

Argenti, Paul, MacDonald, Maril, and O'Neill, Sean (2018). The evolving corporate communication function. In Roger Bolton, Don W. Stacks, and Eliot Mizrachi (Eds.), The New Era of the CCO, *The Essential Role of Communication in a Volatile World* (pp. 19–34). New York, NY: Business Expert Press.

Bettag, Larry (2014). *No rewind, only one shot*. Bloomington, IN: WestBow press.

Blok, Mark (2013). *Breaking Corporate Silence* (Executive Master's thesis). Rotterdam, Netherlands: Rotterdam Business School.

Bourne, Lynda (2006, July). *Project Relationships and the Stakeholder Circle*. Presented at the PMI Research Conference, Montreal, Canada. Retrieved from www. mosaicprojects.com.au

Browne, John, and Nuttall, Robin (2013, March). Beyond corporate social responsibility: Integrated external engagement. *McKinsey Quarterly*. Retrieved from http://www. mckinsey.com/business-functions/strategy- and-corporate-finance/our-insights/beyond- corporate-social-responsibility-integrated- external-engagement

Collins, Jim, and Porras, Jerry I. (1966/2011). Building your company's vision. *Harvard Business Review*, 74, 65–77. Re-published in HBR (2011). *HBR's 10 Must Reads On Strategy* (pp. 77-102). Boston, MA: Harvard Business School Publishing Corporation.

Edmondson, Amy C. (2012, April). Teamwork on the fly, *Harvard Business Review*, 90, 72–80.

Eisenhower, Dwight D. (1954, August). Address at the Second Assembly of the World Council of Churches, Evanston, Illinois. Retrieved from Gerhard Peters and John T. Woolley, The American Presidency Project. http://www.presidency.ucsb.edu/ ws/?pid=9991

Freeman, R. Edward (1984/2010). Strategic Management: *A Stakeholder Approach*. New York, NY: Cambridge University Press.

Geursen, Goos (2006). *Als de leuning beweegt* [When the support moves]. Zalt- bommel, Netherlands: Uitgeverij Thema.

Gray, Dave, & Van der Wal, Thomas (2012). *The connected company*. Sebastopol, CA: O'Reilly Media Inc.

Habermas, Jürgen. (1962). *Strukturwandel der Oeffentlichkeit. Untersuchungen zu einer Kategorie der bürgerlichen Gesellschaft* [The Structural Transformation of the Public Sphere]. Darmstadt, Germany: Luchterhand.

Holyoak, Keith J. (1991). Symbolic connectionism: Toward third-generation theories of expertise. In K. Anders Ericsson and Jacqui Smith (Eds.), *Toward a General Theory of Expertise: Prospects and Limits* (pp. 301–335). New York: Cambridge University Press.

Jamous, H., and Peloille, B. (1970). Professions or self-perpetuating system; changes in the French University-Hospital ystem. In J. A. Jackson (Ed.), *Professions and Professionalization* (pp. 109–152). Cambridge, England: Cambridge University Press.

Keller, Scott, and Price, Collin (2011). Beyond Performance. *How Great Organizations Build Ultimate Competitive Advantage*. Hoboken, NJ: John Wiley & Sons.

Körver, Frank (2012). Een afdeling met impact [A department with impact]. In Betteke van Ruler (Ed.), *Communicatie NU* [Communication NOW] (pp. 54–57). Amsterdam, Netherlands: Adfo Groep.

Koten, John A. (2004). Introduction. In *Building Trust. Leading CEOs Speak Out* (pp. xi-xxiii). New York, NY: Arthur W. Page Society.

Macnamara, Jim (2016). *Organizational Listening. The Missing Essential in Public Communication*. New York, NY: Peter Lang.

Maister, David, Green, Charles, and Galford, Robert (2002). *The Trusted Advisor*. New York, NY: Simon & Schuster.

Martin, Roger L. (2014, January–February). The big lie of strategic planning. A detailed plan may be comforting, but it's not a strategy. *Harvard Business Review*, 92, 78–84.

McKeown, Max (2016). *The Strategy Book* (2nd edition). Harlow, England: Pearson.

Minto, Barbara (2008). *The Pyramid Principle. Logic in Writing and Thinking*. New York, NY: Financial Times Prentice Hall.

Mintzberg, Henry, and Waters, James A. (1985). Of strategies, deliberate and emergent. *Strategic Management Journal*, 6(3), 257-272.

Mintzberg, Henry, Ahlstrand, Bruce, and Lampel, Joseph (2005). *On Strategy Safari. A Guided Tour Through the Wilds of Strategic Management*. New York, NY: The Free Press.

Mintzberg, Henry, Quinn, James Brian, and Ghoshal, Sumantra (2013). *The Strategy Process*. London, England: Prentice-Hall.

Mitchell, Ronald K., Agle, Bradley R., and Wood, Donna J. (1997). Toward a theory of stakeholder identification and salience: Defining the principle of who and what really counts. *The Academy of Management Review*, 22(4), 853-886.

John Naisbitt Quotes. (n.d.). BrainyQuote. com. Retrieved March 18, 2018, from BrainyQuote.com Web site: https://www.brainy-quote.com/quotes/john_naisbitt_384654

Nothhaft, Howard (2010). Communication management as a second-order management function: Roles and functions of the communication executive—results from a shadowing study. *Journal of Communication Management*, 14(2), 127–140.

Parkinson, Cyril (1958). *Parkinson's Law: The Pursuit of Progress.* London, England: John Murray.

Peter, Laurence J., and Hull, Raymond (1969). *The Peter Principle: Why Things Always Go Wrong.* New York, NY: William Morrow and Company.

Porter, Michael (2011). What is strategy? In *On Strategy, HBR's 10 Must Reads* (pp.1–37). Boston, MA: Harvard Business Review Press.

Prince, Russ Alan, and Rogers, Bruce (2012). What is a thought leader? *Forbes.* Retrieved from https://www.forbes.com/sites/rus-sprince/2012/03/16/what-is-a-thought-leader/#178cbe317da0

PWC (2012). *The agile enterprise.* Retrieved January 20, 2014, from www.pwc.com

Reeves, Martin, and Deimler, Mike (2011, July–August). Adaptability: The new competitive advantage. *Harvard Business Review.* Retrieved from https://hbr.org/2011/07/adaptability-the-new-competitive-advantage

Remmelzwaal, Carlijn, Wehrmann, Caroline, and Körver, Frank (2015). From output to impact. How to increase the accountability of a communication department by making use of available data within the organization. Proceedings of the CCI Conference, New York.

Reiman, Joey (2013). *The Story of Purpose: The Path to Creating a Brighter Brand, a Greater Company, and a Lasting Legacy.* Hoboken, NJ: John Wiley & Sons.

Roberts, John, and Scapens, Robert (1985). Accounting Systems and Systems of Accountability—Understanding Accounting Practices in their Organisational Contexts. *Accounting, Organizations and Society*, 10(4), pp. 443–456. Cited in: Johansen, T. R. (2008). *Journal of Business Ethics*, 83(2), 247. doi:10.1007/s10551-007-9615-x

Rogers, Everett M. (1995). *Diffusion of Innovations.* New York, NY: Simon & Schuster.

Savage, Grant T., Nix, Timothy W., Whitehead, Carlton J. and Blair, John D. (1991). Strategies for assessing and managing organizational stakeholders. *Academy of Management Executive*, 5(2), 61-75.

Savage, Grant T., Bunn, Michele D., Gray, Barbara, Xiao, Qian, Wang, Sijun, Wilson, Elizabeth J. and Williams, Eric S. (2011). Stakeholder collaboration: Implications for stakeholder theory and practice. *Journal of Business Ethics.* doi:10.1007/s10551-011-0939-1

Schoemaker, Paul J. H., and Day, George S. (2009). Why we miss the signs. *MIT Sloan Management Review*, 50(2), 43–44.

Schön, Donald (1983). *The Reflective Practitioner. How Professionals Think in Action.* London, England: Temple Smith.

Smith, Ronald D. (2013). *Strategic Planning for Public Relations* (4th edition). New York, NY: Routledge.

Taleb, Nassim Nicholas (2007). The Black Swan: *The Impact of the Highly Improbable.* New York, NY: Random House.

Tench, Ralph (2015). Mapping communication management competencies for European practitioners: ECOPSI, an EU study. *Journal of Communication Management*, 19(1), 39–61.

Tench, Ralph, Verčič, Dejan, Zerfass, Ansgar, Moreno, Ángeles, and Verhoeven, Piet (2016). *Communication Excellence. How to Develop, Manage and Lead Exceptional Communications.* Cham, Switzerland: Palgrave Macmillan.

Tuckman, Bruce W. (1965). Developmental sequence in small groups. *Psychological Bulletin*, 63(6), 384–399. Retrieved from http://psycnet.apa.org/record/1965-12187-001

Van Ruler, Betteke (2004). The Communication Grid, introduction of a model of basic communication strategies in public relations practice. *Public Relations Review*, 30(2), 123–143.

Van Ruler, Betteke (2012). *Met het oog op communicatie, reflecties op het communicatievak* [With an eye on communication, reflections on the communication profession]. The Hague, Netherlands: Boom Lemma.

Van Ruler, Betteke (2014). *Reflective Communication Scrum, Recipe for Accountability.* The Hague, Netherlands: Eleven.

Van Ruler, Betteke, and Verčič, Dejan (2008). Communication Management in Europe—Challenges and Opportunities. In Zerfass, Ansgar, Ruler, Betteke van, and Sriramesh, Krishnamurthy (Eds.), *Public Relations Research. European and International Perspectives and Innovations* (pp. 313–324). Wiesbaden, Germany: VS Verlag für Sozialwissenschaften.

Waldock, Belinda (2015). *Being Agile in Business.* Harlow, England: Pearson.

ABOUT
THE
AUTHORS

Betteke van Ruler, Ph.D., is professor emerita of Corporate Communication and Communication Management at the University of Amsterdam and co-owner of The Van Ruler Academy, where professionals learn and meet. In the first 17 years of her career she worked in communication practice, and subsequently embarked on a career as a teacher and scholar. Over the course of her career she has published many books and articles on the theory and practice of communication in both Dutch and English, and she is frequently invited to speak on developments in the communication field. During her academic tenure she was president of the European Public Relations Education and Research Association and chair of the Public Relations Division of the International Communication Association. She is Honorary Fellow of the Amsterdam School of Communications Research and was honored with the prestigious ICA Fellowship award of the International Communication Association (2018).

Frank Körver, M.Sc., is partner at consulting firm Wepublic, based in Amsterdam and The Hague. Wepublic is the Dutch affiliate of the global Interel Group. Frank is trusted advisor of CCOs and other senior-level executives. He is specialized in issues and reputation management, corporate communication strategy and leadership challenges. Many of his clients are organizations experiencing complex reputation challenges and strategic dilemmas, or have the ambition to create an impact-focused communication function. Frank is amongst others board member of the business club of the Cobra museum of modern art and the Dutch co-coordinator of the European Association of Communication Directors (EACD). He previously wrote a book on strategic issues management.

NOTES

NOTES

NOTES